THE ASQ CSSBB STUDY GUIDE

Also available from ASQ Quality Press:

The Certified Six Sigma Black Belt Handbook, Third Edition
T. M. Kubiak and Donald W. Benbow

Practical Engineering, Process, and Reliability Statistics
Mark Allen Durivage

Statistics for Six Sigma Black Belts
Matthew A. Barsalou

The Certified Supplier Quality Professional Handbook
Mark Allen Durivage, editor

The Certified Reliability Engineer Handbook, Third Edition
Mark Allen Durivage, editor

Practical Process Validation
Mark Allen Durivage and Bob (Bhavan) Mehta

The ASQ CQE Study Guide
Connie M. Borror and Sarah E. Burke

The Probability Workbook
Mary McShane-Vaughn

The Certified Quality Engineer Handbook, Fourth Edition
Sarah E. Burke and Rachel T. Silvestrini, editor

The Quality Toolbox, Second Edition
Nancy R. Tague

The Certified Six Sigma Green Belt Handbook, Second Edition
Roderick A. Munro, Govindarajan Ramu, and Daniel J. Zrymiak

The Certified Manager of Quality/Organizational Excellence Handbook, Fourth Edition
Russell T. Westcott, editor

To request a complimentary catalog of ASQ Quality Press publications, call 800-248-1946, or visit our website at http://www.asq.org/quality-press.

THE ASQ CSSBB STUDY GUIDE

Mark Allen Durivage
Shawn Findlater

ASQ Quality Press
Milwaukee, Wisconsin

American Society for Quality, Quality Press, Milwaukee 53203
© 2018 by ASQ
All rights reserved. Published 2017
Printed in the United States of America
25 24 23 22 21 HP 10 9 8 7 6

Library of Congress Cataloging-in-Publication Data

Names: Durivage, Mark Allen, author. | Findlater, Shawn, author. | American
Society for Quality, issuing body.
Title: The ASQ CSSBB study guide / Mark Allen Durivage, Shawn Findlater.
Description: Milwaukee, Wisconsin : ASQ Quality Press, [2017] | Includes
bibliographical references and index.
Identifiers: LCCN 2017033367 | ISBN 9780873899611 (softcover : alk. paper)
Subjects: LCSH: Six sigma (Quality control standard)—Examinations—Study
guides.
Classification: LCC TS156.17.S59 D87 2017 | DDC 658.5/620218—dc23
LC record available at https://lccn.loc.gov/2017033367

ISBN: 978-0-87389-961-1

ASQ Mission: The American Society for Quality advances individual, organizational, and community
excellence worldwide through learning, quality improvement, and knowledge exchange.

Attention Bookstores, Wholesalers, Schools, and Corporations: ASQ Quality Press books, video,
audio, and software are available at quantity discounts with bulk purchases for business, educational,
or instructional use. For information, please contact ASQ Quality Press at 800-248-1946, or write to
ASQ Quality Press, P.O. Box 3005, Milwaukee, WI 53201-3005.

To place orders or to request ASQ membership information, call 800-248-1946. Visit our website at
http://www.asq.org/quality-press.

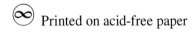 Printed on acid-free paper

Quality Press
600 N. Plankinton Ave.
Milwaukee, WI 53203-2914
E-mail: authors@asq.org
ASQ **The Global Voice of Quality®**

*I would like to dedicate this book to and recognize the patience
of my wife Dawn and my sons Jack and Sam, which allowed me time to
complete this project. I would also like to thank Shawn Findlater for
partnering on this project, and in the process becoming my friend.*

—*Mark Allen Durivage*

*To my amazing wife Nathalie for having patience with me and taking the lion's
share of the home tasks, allowing me to finish this book. I love you.
To my full-of-potential daughters, Camille and Alexa, I hope to inspire you
to never let any status quo stop you from achieving your dreams.*

—*Shawn Findlater*

Table of Contents

Introduction

This book is primarily meant to aid those taking the ASQ Certified Six Sigma Black Belt (CSSBB) exam, and is best used in conjunction with *The Certified Six Sigma Black Belt Handbook* (ASQ Quality Press). Section 1 provides over 430 practice questions organized by the nine parts of the 2015 Body of Knowledge (BoK). Section 2 gives the reader a 150-question practice exam comprising each of the nine parts of the BoK, in a randomized order that simulates the actual certification exam.

Unlike other resources on the market, all these questions and solutions were developed specifically to address the 2015 CSSBB Body of Knowledge and help those studying for the certification, including considering the proper depth of knowledge and required levels of cognition.

Please note that all calculations for these questions were performed using a simple scientific calculator. Therefore, some answers may vary slightly if worked with a spreadsheet or other software application. The authors strongly suggest referring to the official ASQ calculator requirements,* purchase a compliant calculator, and practice using the calculator. Additionally, we suggest purchasing the *Certified Six Sigma Black Belt Handbook* from ASQ Quality Press and becoming familiar with the equations and statistical tables provided in the appendixes in order to optimize your time during the actual certification exam.

As a reminder, practice/sample test questions such as those in this study guide cannot be taken into ASQ certification exam rooms. The certification exam is open book. It is strongly recommended that you do take the *Certified Six Sigma Black Belt Handbook* in with you to look up or verify any answers as you work the exam questions.

We welcome your feedback and suggestions for improvement. Please contact us at authors@asq.org and we will do our best to clarify any questions you may have and incorporate any suggestions for improvement into future printings or editions of this study guide.

Mark Durivage
Lambertville, Michigan

Shawn Findlater
Fort Lauderdale, Florida

https://asq.org/cert/faq/calculator

Acknowledgments

The *ASQ CSSBB Study Guide* is dedicated to the hardworking individuals globally who work tirelessly for their companies to improve and optimize service and production processes.

We would like to acknowledge Sara Deem and Chad Walters for their very thorough and detailed review of the draft manuscript.

We would like to thank those who have inspired, taught, and trained us throughout our professional careers. Additionally, we would like to thank ASQ Quality Press, especially Paul O'Mara, Managing Editor, and Randy Benson, Senior Creative Services Specialist, for their expertise and technical competence, which made this project a reality.

LIMIT OF LIABILITY/DISCLAIMER OF WARRANTY

The authors have put forth their best effort in compiling the content of this book; however, no warranty with respect to the material's accuracy or completeness is made. Additionally, no warranty is made in regard to applying the recommendations made in this book to any business structure or environments. Businesses should consult regulatory, quality, and/or legal professionals prior to deciding on the appropriateness of advice and recommendations made within this book. The authors shall not be held liable for loss of profit or other commercial damages resulting from the employment of recommendations made within this book, including special, incidental, consequential, or other damages.

Section 1
Practice Questions

This section is divided into nine parts, one for each section in the Certified Six Sigma Black Belt (CSSBB) Body of Knowledge (BoK). In each part, there is a set of questions followed by detailed solutions.

Part I

Organization-Wide Planning and Deployment

(30 questions)

A. ORGANIZATION-WIDE CONSIDERATIONS

1. *Fundamentals of six sigma and lean methodologies.* Define and describe the value, foundations, philosophy, history, and goals of these approaches, and describe the integration and complementary relationship between them. (Understand)

2. *Six sigma, lean, and continuous improvement methodologies.* Describe when to use six sigma instead of other problem-solving approaches, and describe the importance of aligning six sigma objectives with organizational goals. Describe screening criteria and how such criteria can be used for the selection of six sigma projects, lean initiatives, and other continuous improvement methods. (Apply)

3. *Relationships among business systems and processes.* Describe the interactive relationships among business systems, processes, and internal and external stakeholders, and the impact those relationships have on business systems. (Understand)

4. *Strategic planning and deployment for initiatives.* Define the importance of strategic planning for six sigma projects and lean initiatives. Demonstrate how hoshin kanri (X-matrix), portfolio analysis, and other tools can be used in support of strategic deployment of these projects. Use feasibility studies, SWOT analysis (strengths, weaknesses, opportunities, and threats), PEST analysis (political, economic, social, and technological) and contingency planning and business continuity planning to enhance strategic planning and deployment. (Apply)

B. LEADERSHIP

1. *Roles and responsibilities.* Describe the roles and responsibilities of executive leadership, champions, sponsors, process owners, master black belts, black belts, and green belts in driving six sigma and lean initiatives. Describe how each group influences project deployment in terms of providing or managing resources, enabling changes in organizational structure, and supporting communications about the purpose and deployment of the initiatives. (Understand)

2. *Organizational roadblocks and change management.* Describe how an organization's structure and culture can impact six sigma projects. Identify common causes of six sigma failures, including lack of management support and lack of resources. Apply change management techniques, including stakeholder analysis, readiness assessments, and communication plans to overcome barriers and drive organization-wide change. (Apply)

QUESTIONS

1. Which quality guru is known as the "father" of statistical quality control?

   a. W. Edwards Deming

   b. Joseph M. Juran

   c. Walter A. Shewhart

   d. Armand V. Feigenbaum

2. Which quality guru developed the cause-and-effect diagram?

   a. Kaoru Ishikawa

   b. Genichi Taguchi

   c. Armand V. Feigenbaum

   d. F. M. Gryna

3. Quality planning, quality control, and quality improvement are part of:

   a. W. Edwards Deming's 14 points.

   b. W. Edwards Deming's 7 deadly sins of quality.

   c. Joseph M. Juran's quality trilogy.

   d. F. M. Gryna's quality trilogy.

4. Which quality guru is responsible for the concept of zero defects?

   a. Armand V. Feigenbaum

   b. Philip B. Crosby

   c. W. Edwards Deming

   d. Genichi Taguchi

5. Who is credited with the concept of total quality?

   a. Armand V. Feigenbaum

   b. F. M. Gryna

   c. Kaoru Ishikawa

   d. Joseph M. Juran

6. Where were quality circles initially used?

    a. Japan

    b. China

    c. United States

    d. Brazil

7. Benchmarking is defined as:

    a. the application of statistical techniques to control a process.

    b. an improvement process in which a company measures its performance against that of best-in-class companies and processes.

    c. self-improvement study groups composed of a small number of employees.

    d. a breakthrough approach involving the restructuring of an entire organization and its processes.

8. Which quality guru taught that any departure from the nominal or target value for a characteristic represents a loss to society?

    a. Kaoru Ishikawa

    b. W. Edwards Deming

    c. F. M. Gryna

    d. Genichi Taguchi

9. Lean Six Sigma:

    a. was established by the U.S. Congress in 1987 to raise awareness of quality management.

    b. combines the individual concepts of lean and Six Sigma.

    c. is a management concept that helps managers at all levels monitor results.

    d. was developed by the Toyota Motor Company.

10. Armand V. Feigenbaum's concept of total quality includes:

    a. quality leadership, modern quality technology, and organizational commitment.

    b. commitment to quality, management commitment, and measure potential quality problems.

   c. statistical process control.

   d. benchmarking and reengineering.

11. Which quality management and quality assurance principle was developed to help companies effectively document the quality system?

   a. Quality circles

   b. Benchmarking

   c. Baldrige Award criteria

   d. ISO 9000

12. The Baldrige Award criteria:

   a. is required for Lean Six Sigma.

   b. is used for ISO 9000 certification.

   c. is used for statistical process control.

   d. raises awareness of quality management.

13. Which quality tool is used to diagram a process?

   a. Control chart

   b. Measles chart

   c. Flowchart

   d. Venn diagram

14. What is the relationship between a process and a system?

   a. Processes are system outputs.

   b. Systems are a series of interrelated processes.

   c. Systems are process inputs.

   d. Processes are a series of interrelated systems.

15. Subprocesses can be broken into:

   a. systems.

   b. steps.

   c. processes.

   d. services.

16. Which quality tool is best used for stating and developing objectives?

    a. Hoshin kanri

    b. Portfolio analysis

    c. SWOT analysis

    d. Risk analysis

17. Which of the following tools would be the most appropriate for keeping management apprised of emerging technologies?

    a. SWOT analysis

    b. PEST analysis

    c. Portfolio analysis

    d. Risk analysis

18. Which of the following tools would be the most appropriate for crisis management?

    a. PEST analysis

    b. SWOT analysis

    c. Contingency planning

    d. Risk analysis

19. A Black Belt is usually associated with an individual who:

    a. is typically assigned full-time to train, mentor, and lead the strategy for chartering organizations' strategic projects.

    b. retains their regular position, but is trained in the tools, methods, and skills necessary to conduct Six Sigma improvement projects.

    c. is typically assigned full-time to train, mentor, and lead improvement projects.

    d. has the authority or ability to make changes in the process as required.

20. A Master Black Belt is usually associated with an individual who:

    a. retains their regular position, but is trained in the tools, methods, and skills necessary to conduct Six Sigma improvement projects.

    b. is typically assigned full-time to train, mentor, and lead improvement projects.

c. is typically assigned full-time to train, mentor, and lead the strategy for chartering organizations' strategic projects.

d. has the authority or ability to make changes in the process as required.

21. A Green Belt is usually associated with an individual who:

a. retains their regular position, but is trained in the tools, methods, and skills necessary to conduct Six Sigma improvement projects.

b. is typically assigned full-time to train, mentor, and lead improvement projects.

c. is typically assigned full-time to train, mentor, and lead the strategy for chartering organizations' strategic projects.

d. has the authority or ability to make changes in the process as required.

22. A *process owner* is usually associated with an individual who:

a. retains their regular position, but is trained in the tools, methods, and skills necessary to conduct Six Sigma improvement projects.

b. is typically assigned full-time to train, mentor, and lead improvement projects.

c. is typically assigned full-time to train, mentor, and lead the strategy for chartering organizations' strategic projects.

d. has the authority or ability to make changes in the process as required.

23. Organizational goals must be consistent with the long-term strategies of the enterprise. One technique for developing such strategies is called:

a. SWOT analysis.

b. PEST analysis.

c. hoshin kanri.

d. DMAIC.

24. A *champion* is usually associated with an individual who:

a. ensures that their projects are aligned with the organization's strategic goals and priorities and removes organizational barriers.

b. retains their regular position, but is trained in the tools, methods, and skills necessary to conduct Six Sigma improvement projects.

c. is typically assigned full-time to train, mentor, and lead improvement projects.

d. is typically assigned full-time to train, mentor, and lead the strategy for chartering organizations' strategic projects.

25. The type of organizational structure that is most resistant to change is:

a. matrix.

b. cross-functional.

c. centralized.

d. decentralized.

26. Effective communication is essential to successfully implementing change. What is typically the first step in this process?

a. Communicate the need for change.

b. Communicate a view of a future state.

c. Communicate goals and metrics.

d. Communicate new policies.

27. Which of the following models is the best for identifying stakeholders of a proposed change in a manufacturing process?

a. SIPOC

b. PDCA

c. DMAIC

d. DFSS

28. The C in the SIPOC model refers to:

a. contractors.

b. customers.

c. currency.

d. capability.

29. The _____ is often the person best able to break roadblocks when implementing change.

a. Black Belt

b. Master Black Belt

   c. manager

   d. champion

30. To maintain support throughout the change life cycle, the organization must:

   a. provide frequent communications.

   b. appoint a management representative.

   c. delegate the responsibilities to a qualified consultant.

   d. divide the responsibility and authority equally between management and the workers.

ANSWERS

1. c; Walter A. Shewhart successfully brought together the disciplines of statistics, engineering, and economics and became known as the father of modern quality control. [I.A.1]

2. a; Kaoru Ishikawa is probably best known for the cause-and-effect diagram—often called the *Ishikawa diagram*. [I.A.1]

3. c; Juran developed the *Juran trilogy*: three managerial processes—quality planning, quality control, and quality improvement—for use in managing for quality. [I.A.1]

4. b; Philip B. Crosby was a legend in the discipline of quality. He is widely recognized for promoting the concept of "zero defects" and for defining quality as *conformance to requirements*. [I.A.1]

5. a; The name Armand V. Feigenbaum and the term "total quality control" are virtually synonymous. [I.A.1]

6. a; Kaoru Ishikawa played a key role in the development of a specifically Japanese quality strategy—*quality circles*. [I.A.1]

7. b; An improvement process in which a company measures its performance against that of best-in-class companies, determines how those companies achieved their performance levels, and uses the information to improve its own performance. The areas that can be benchmarked include strategies, operations, processes, and procedures. [I.A.2]

8. d; Genichi Taguchi taught that any departure from the nominal or target value for a characteristic represents a loss to society. [I.A.1]

9. b; This approach combines the individual concepts of lean and Six Sigma and recognizes that both are necessary to effectively drive sustained improvement. [I.A.2]

10. a; Armand V. Feigenbaum lists three steps to quality: quality leadership, modern quality technology, and organizational commitment. [I.A.1]

11. d; The ISO standards are a set of international standards on quality management and quality assurance developed to help companies effectively document the quality system elements to be implemented to maintain an efficient quality system. [I.A.2]

12. d; The Baldrige Award was established by the U.S. Congress in 1987 to raise awareness of quality management and recognize U.S. companies that have implemented successful quality management systems. [I.A.1]

13. c; *Flowcharts* are graphical representations of the steps in a process. Flowcharts are drawn to better understand processes. [I.A.3]

14. b; A *system* is group of interdependent processes and people that together perform a common mission. [I.A.3]

15. b; Systems are hierarchical and comprise processes, subprocesses, and steps. Each part of a system can be broken into a series of processes, each of which may have subprocesses. The subprocesses may be further broken into steps. [I.A.3]

16. a; Hoshin kanri planning provides tools for stating objectives for the organization and managing their implementation. [I.A.4]

17. b; A SWOT (strengths, weaknesses, opportunities, and threats) analysis is an effective strategic planning tool applicable to a business or project objective. Strengths and weaknesses are identified with respect to the internal capabilities of an organization, while opportunities and threats look outside the organization to identify opportunities for the organization and threats to the organization. [I.A.4]

18. c; Contingency planning (also called a *plan B*) is used for crisis management, business continuity, and asset security. [I.A.4]

19. c; Black Belt (BB)—A Six Sigma role associated with an individual typically assigned full-time to train and mentor Green Belts as well as lead improvement projects using specified methodologies such as DMAIC (define, measure, analyze, improve, control), DMADV (define, measure, analyze, design, verify), and DFSS (design for Six Sigma). [I.B.1]

20 c; Master Black Belt (MBB)—A Six Sigma role associated with an individual typically assigned full-time to train and mentor Black Belts as well as lead the strategy to ensure that the improvement projects chartered are the right strategic projects for the organization. Master Black Belts are usually the authorizing body to certify Green Belts and Black Belts. [I.B.1]

21. a; Green Belt (GB)—A Six Sigma role associated with an individual who retains his or her regular position within the firm but is trained in the tools, methods, and skills necessary to conduct Six Sigma improvement projects either individually or as part of larger teams. [I.B.1]

22. d; Process owner—A Six Sigma role associated with an individual who coordinates the various functions and work activities at all levels of a process, has the authority or ability to make changes in the process as required, and manages the entire process cycle so as to ensure performance effectiveness. [I.B.1]

23. c; Hoshin kanri planning provides tools for stating objectives for the organization and managing their implementation. [I.B.1]

24. a; Champion—A Six Sigma role associated with a senior manager who ensures that his or her projects are aligned with the organization's strategic goals and priorities, provides the Six Sigma team with resources, removes organizational barriers for the team, participates in project tollgate reviews, and essentially serves as the team's backer. A champion is also known as a *sponsor.* [I.B.1]

25. c; A highly centralized organizational structure tends to resist any change, and fundamental improvements are difficult to achieve. [I.B.2]

26. a; Effective communication is considered essential for success. Communicating the need for change is the first step in the change management process. [I.B.2]

27. a; Suppliers–inputs–process–outputs–customers (SIPOC) can be used to identify stakeholders. [I.B.2]

28. b; Suppliers–inputs–process–outputs–customers (SIPOC). [I.B.2]

29. d; Champion—A Six Sigma role associated with a senior manager who ensures that his or her projects are aligned with the organization's strategic goals and priorities, provides the Six Sigma team with resources, removes organizational barriers for the team, participates in project tollgate reviews, and essentially serves as the team's backer. A champion is also known as a *sponsor.* [I.B.2]

30. a; Continuous communication of project status throughout the change cycle is the key to maintaining support. [I.B.2]

Part II

Organizational Process Management and Measures

(26 questions)

A. IMPACT ON STAKEHOLDERS

Describe the impact six sigma projects can have on customers, suppliers, and other stakeholders. (Understand)

B. BENCHMARKING

Define and distinguish between various types of benchmarking, e.g., best practices, competitive, collaborative, breakthrough. Select measures and performance goals for projects resulting from benchmarking activities. (Apply)

C. BUSINESS MEASURES

1. *Performance measures.* Define and describe balanced scorecard, key performance indicators (KPIs), customer loyalty metrics, and leading and lagging indicators. Explain how to create a line of sight from performance measures to organizational strategies. (Analyze)

2. *Financial measures.* Define and use revenue growth, market share, margin, net present value (NPV), return on investment (ROI), and cost–benefit analysis (CBA). Explain the difference between hard cost measures (from profit and loss statements) and soft cost benefits of cost avoidance and reduction. (Apply)

QUESTIONS

1. Supporting, opposing, helping, and hindering are:

   a. four features that affect stakeholders.

   b. four steps of stakeholder analysis.

   c. types of stakeholders.

   d. analysis planning steps.

2. Any individual or group with an interest in the business is considered a/an:

   a. stakeholder.

   b. shareholder.

   c. regulator.

   d. employee.

3. One of the most common tools used to identify stakeholders is:

   a. DFSS.

   b. DMAIC.

   c. SIPOC.

   d. PDCA.

4. Identifying the issue to be addressed and the necessary actions is the:

   a. shareholder analytical process.

   b. stakeholders analytical process.

   c. stakeholders analysis.

   d. shareholder analysis.

5. Delivering the right level of information, to the right stakeholders, at the right time is part of the:

   a. company newsletter.

   b. company annual report.

   c. human resources function.

   d. communications management process.

6. Which of the following is a formal or informal communication used to acknowledge a key milestone?

    a. Newsletter

    b. Annual report

    c. Gossip

    d. Announcements

7. Determining the communications needs necessary for the project stakeholders is:

    a. communication theory analysis.

    b. communication management process.

    c. communication management plan.

    d. communication requirements analysis.

8. Organizations usually utilize benchmarking to:

    a. collect and develop data on industry best practices.

    b. perform root cause analysis.

    c. increase market penetration.

    d. determine critical-to-quality features.

9. Which of the following is the first step a company should take in benchmarking?

    a. Incorporate best practices

    b. Redesign customer concepts

    c. Collect external data

    d. Collect internal data

10. An organization would use which tool to evaluate competitive processes?

    a. Customer survey

    b. Hoshin planning

    c. Benchmarking

    d. Affinity diagram

11. A comparison of best practices in other industries to facilitate process performance is referred to as:

    a. benchmarking.

    b. process mapping.

    c. stakeholder analysis.

    d. monitoring.

12. The act of conducting performance or process benchmarking within an organization by comparing similar business units or business processes is:

    a. functional benchmarking.

    b. internal benchmarking.

    c. strategic benchmarking.

    d. focused benchmarking.

13. The benchmarking process can be ineffective if the process:

    a. has not been fully defined.

    b. is fully mapped.

    c. is not industry specific.

    d. was provided by a consultant.

14. The benchmarking process usually follows which sequence?

    a. Presentation, data collection, statistical analysis, and planning

    b. Presentation, analysis, and implementation

    c. Planning, data collection, analysis, and implementation

    d. Planning, detection factors, statistical analysis, and integration

15. Kaplan and Norton coined the concept of the *balanced scorecard*. A balanced scorecard does not include information from:

    a. stockholders.

    b. processes.

    c. financials.

    d. customers.

16. Which perspective provides shareholders with a direct line of sight into the health and well-being of the organization?

    a. Financial perspective

    b. Customer perspective

    c. Internal business processes perspective

    d. Learning and growth perspective

17. Which perspective includes the capabilities and skills of an organization?

    a. Financial perspective

    b. Learning and growth perspective

    c. Internal business processes perspective

    d. Customer perspective

18. Which perspective defines an organization's value proposition and measures how effective the organization is in creating value?

    a. Internal business processes perspective

    b. Learning and growth perspective

    c. Financial perspective

    d. Customer perspective

19. Which perspective is designed to create and deliver the customer's value proposition?

    a. Financial perspective

    b. Learning and growth perspective

    c. Internal business processes perspective

    d. Customer perspective

20. Which of the following is the least effective way to measure customer loyalty?

    a. Quarterly sales volume

    b. Customer referrals

    c. Customer abandonment rate

    d. Customer retention rate

21. In five years, $5000 will be available. What is the net present value (NPV) of that money, assuming an annual interest rate of 10%?

    a. $500.00

    b. $1581.14

    c. $3104.61

    d. $5000.00

22. The net present value (NPV) costs to conduct a project are estimated to be $100,000. The NPV benefits or savings due to the project are estimated at $750,000. Compute the benefit-to-cost ratio.

    a. $0.13

    b. $7.50

    c. $100,000

    d. $750,000

23. Costs associated with customer complaints are best characterized as:

    a. appraisal costs.

    b. prevention costs.

    c. internal failure costs.

    d. external failure costs.

24. The costs associated with acceptance sampling are:

    a. appraisal costs.

    b. prevention costs.

    c. internal failure costs.

    d. external failure costs.

25. The costs associated with the operation and activities of the material review board (MRB) are:

    a. appraisal costs.

    b. prevention costs.

    c. internal failure costs.

    d. external failure costs.

26. The costs associated with the implementation of a company-wide training initiative are:

    a. appraisal costs.

    b. prevention costs.

    c. internal failure costs.

    d. external failure costs.

ANSWERS

1. c; There are four types of stakeholders. Stakeholders can be supporting, opposing, helping, or hindering. [II.A]

2. a; *Stakeholder* is defined as anyone with an interest or right in an issue , or anyone who can affect or be affected by an action or change. [II.A]

3. c; Suppliers–inputs–process–outputs–customers (SIPOC) is a process mapping method that is used to take a high-level view of a specific process, identify stakeholders, and determine where improvements can be made. [II.A]

4. b; The stakeholder analytical process is used to identify the issues to be addressed and the necessary actions. [II.A]

5. d; The communication management process ensures delivering the right level of information, to the right stakeholders, at the right time. [II.A]

6. d; Announcements (formal or informal) are communications used to acknowledge a key milestone. [II.A]

7. d; Communications requirements analysis is used to determine the communications needs necessary for the project stakeholders. [II.A]

8. c; Benchmarking provides an organization with the opportunity to see what level of process performance is possible. [II.B]

9. d; It is important to collect internal data prior to collecting external data when an organization decides to benchmark. [II.B]

10. c; Competitive benchmarking forces organizations to take an external perspective. [II.B]

11. a; Generic benchmarking is the act of comparing the processes or performance of two or more companies irrespective of their industries. [II.B]

12. b; Internal benchmarking is the act of conducting performance or process benchmarking within an organization by comparing similar business units or business processes. [II.B]

13. a; Benchmarking requires the use of a strict methodology. It must be planned and funded or it will likely fail. [II.B]

14. c; The benchmarking process follows the PDCA cycle: planning, data collection, analysis, and implementation. [II.B]

15. a; Kaplan and Norton (1996) coined the phrase *balanced scorecard*, consisting of the following perspectives: financial, customer, internal business processes, and learning and growth. [II.C.1]

16. a; The financial perspective provides shareholders with a direct line of sight into the health and well-being of the organization. [II.C.1]

17. b; The learning and growth perspective includes the capabilities and skills of an organization and how they are focused and channeled to support the internal processes used to create customer value. [II.C.1]

18. d; The customer perspective defines an organization's value proposition, and measures how effective the organization is in creating value for its customers through its goals, objectives, strategies, and processes. [II.C.1]

19. c; The internal business processes perspective includes all organizational processes designed to create and deliver the customer's value proposition. [II.C.1]

20. a; Customer loyalty is best measured by the following metrics: customer referrals, customer abandonment rates, and customer retention rates. [II.C.1]

21. c; In five years, $5000 will be available. The net present value of that money, assuming an annual interest rate of 10% can be calculated by

$$P = F(1 + i)^{-n}$$

where

P = Net present value

F = Amount to be received n years from now

i = Annual interest rate expressed as a decimal

[II.C.2]

22. b; The net present value (NPV) costs to conduct a project are estimated to be $100,000. The NPV benefits or savings due to the project are estimated at $750,000. The benefit-to-cost ratio can be calculated by

$$\frac{\Sigma \text{ NPV of all benefits anticipated}}{\Sigma \text{ NPV of all costs anticipated}} = \frac{\$750,000}{\$100,000} = \$7.50$$

[II.C.2]

23. d; External failure costs are costs incurred when a failure occurs while the customer owns the product. [II.C.2]

24. a; Appraisal costs are costs associated with the inspection and appraisal processes. [II.C.2]

25. c; Internal failure costs are costs incurred when a failure occurs in-house, and are usually associated with the cost of scrap and rework. [II.C.2]

26. b; Prevention costs are the costs of all activities whose purpose is to prevent failures, including training, quality planning, and quality control activities. [II.C.2]

Part III

Team Management

(40 questions)

A. TEAM FORMATION

1. *Team types and constraints.* Define and describe various teams, including virtual, cross-functional, and self-directed. Determine what team type will work best for a given set of constraints, e.g., geography, technology availability, staff schedules, time zones. (Apply)

2. *Team roles and responsibilities.* Define and describe various team roles and responsibilities for leader, facilitator, coach, and individual member. (Understand)

3. *Team member selection criteria.* Describe various factors that influence the selection of team members, including the ability to influence, openness to change, required skills sets, subject matter expertise, and availability. (Apply)

4. *Team success factors.* Identify and describe the elements necessary for successful teams, e.g., management support, clear goals, ground rules, timelines. (Apply)

B. TEAM FACILITATION

1. *Motivational techniques.* Describe and apply techniques to motivate team members. Identify factors that can demotivate team members and describe techniques to overcome them. (Apply)

2. *Team stages of development.* Identify and describe the classic stages of team development: forming, storming, norming, performing, and adjourning. (Apply)

3. *Team communication.* Describe and explain the elements of an effective communication plan, e.g., audience identification, message type, medium, frequency. (Apply)

4. *Team leadership models.* Describe and select appropriate leadership approaches (e.g., direct, coach, support, delegate) to ensure team success. (Apply)

C. TEAM DYNAMICS

1. *Group behaviors.* Identify and use various conflict resolution techniques (e.g., coaching, mentoring, intervention) to overcome negative group dynamics, including dominant and reluctant participants, groupthink, rushing to finish, and digressions. (Evaluate)

2. *Meeting management.* Select and use various meeting management techniques, including using agendas, starting on time, requiring pre-work by attendees, and ensuring that the right people and resources are available. (Apply)

3. *Team decision-making methods.* Define, select, and use various tools (e.g., consensus, nominal group technique, multi-voting) for decision-making. (Apply)

D. TEAM TRAINING

1. *Needs assessment.* Identify the steps involved to implement an effective training curriculum: identify skills gaps, develop learning objectives, prepare a training plan, and develop training materials. (Understand)

2. *Delivery.* Describe various techniques used to deliver effective training, including adult learning theory, soft skills, and modes of learning. (Understand)

3. *Evaluation.* Describe various techniques to evaluate training, including evaluation planning, feedback surveys, pre-training and post-training testing. (Understand)

QUESTIONS

1. Which team type of improvement is the least affected by geography?

   a. Cross-directional

   b. Self-directed

   c. Virtual

   d. Visual

2. This individual does not generally attend regular Six Sigma project team meetings.

   a. Facilitator

   b. Team leader

   c. Coach

   d. Champion

3. An improvement project team coach is usually responsible for:

   a. maintaining and publishing meeting minutes.

   b. summarizing progress using visual aids.

   c. notifying the team leader or facilitator of the time remaining on each agenda item.

   d. working with the team leader and facilitator to move the team toward the objective, and monitoring team progress.

4. A good Six Sigma project team member is characterized by:

   a. being politically correct.

   b. avoiding constructive debate.

   c. being on time.

   d. fostering concurrent discussions.

5. A company has formed a team that has members with diverse roles and skill sets. This type of team is best defined as:

   a. virtual reality.

   b. process improvement.

   c. cross-functional.

   d. self-directed.

6. Process improvement teams should have training on which of the following topics?

    a. Process dynamics

    b. Team building

    c. Project management

    d. Program management

7. A Six Sigma team with specific goals linked to the organization's strategic objectives is called a/an:

    a. advisory team.

    b. virtual team.

    c. informal team.

    d. formal team.

8. The individual responsible for organizing, hosting, and running the team meeting is the:

    a. champion.

    b. sponsor.

    c. mentor.

    d. leader.

9. The person providing assistance when necessary to individual team members to assure that action items are completed is the:

    a. coach.

    b. champion.

    c. leader.

    d. facilitator.

10. A cross-divisional Six Sigma improvement team from different locations that may not meet in person is a:

    a. virtual team.

    b. informal team.

    c. formal team.

    d. ineffective team.

11. The team phase where team members struggle to understand the team goal and its meaning for them individually is referred to as:

    a. forming.

    b. storming.

    c. norming.

    d. performing.

12. The team phase where team members begin to understand the need to operate as a team rather than as a group of individuals is referred to as:

    a. forming.

    b. storming.

    c. norming.

    d. performing.

13. The team phase where team members express their own opinions and ideas, often disagreeing with others, is referred to as:

    a. forming.

    b. storming.

    c. norming.

    d. performing.

14. The team phase where team members understand one another and recognize each other's strengths and weaknesses is referred to as:

    a. performing.

    b. forming.

    c. storming.

    d. norming.

15. A high-performing team has recently had changes to the individuals participating in the team project. With the change in personnel, in what stage is the team likely to find itself?

    a. Storming

    b. Forming

    c. Norming

    d. Performing

16. A process improvement team has just made a significant breakthrough. The plant manager formally recognizes the achievement during an all-employee meeting. This is an example of:

    a. rewards.

    b. product realization.

    c. individual performance.

    d. recognition.

17. Interactions between team members that result in improved operation are:

    a. functional commitment.

    b. team forming.

    c. effective individual communication.

    d. effective team communication.

18. The type of leader who provides clear direction to team members is:

    a. supportive.

    b. coaching.

    c. situational.

    d. directional.

19. A leader empowering process improvement team members to function independently is known as _____ leadership.

    a. situational

    b. supportive

    c. deductive

    d. directional

20. What type of leadership is best suited for high-performing team members that are technically competent?

    a. Delegating

    b. Directional

    c. Supportive

    d. Adversarial

21. The primary difference between a coach and mentor can best be described as:

    a. coaches usually work with individuals to develop skills and abilities.

    b. mentors usually work with teams to develop skills and abilities.

    c. mentors help projects stay on track and advance toward completion in a timely manner.

    d. coaches provide guidance and direction on how to navigate organizational barriers.

22. A project team has discussed several possible solutions based on data provided by the process owner. The team has reached agreement on the course of action. This agreement is called:

    a. consensus.

    b. purpose.

    c. planning.

    d. agenda.

23. _____ are usually developed when a team is formed.

    a. Objectives

    b. Goals

    c. Ground rules

    d. Metrics

24. When a team member decides not to express their opinion because they are fearful of alienating others in the group, this is known as:

    a. groupthink.

    b. brainstorming.

    c. confirmation.

    d. invulnerability.

25. When a team shares information, and uses data to make decisions and coordinate action, this is referred to as:

    a. action items.

    b. meeting functions.

    c. symptoms of groupthink.

    d. actions to avoid groupthink.

26. When a Six Sigma process improvement team has pooled their collective expertise to develop a solution, this is referred to as:

    a. coordination.

    b. decision making.

    c. groupthink.

    d. action items.

27. When teams do not make hasty decisions, and are open to criticism, these are considered:

    a. action items.

    b. meeting functions.

    c. symptoms of groupthink.

    d. actions to avoid groupthink.

28. A technique for the generation of ideas where ideas are written down without any discussion, after which the ideas are ranked is:

    a. brainstorming.

    b. affinity analysis.

    c. nominal group technique.

    d. configuration management.

29. Brainstorming is most associated with:

    a. generating ideas.

    b. eliminating ideas.

    c. ranking ideas.

    d. reducing ideas.

30. A technique that raises multiple perspectives and counteracts biases is:

    a. nominal group technique.

    b. brainstorming.

    c. affinity analysis.

    d. devil's advocate.

31. The terms "training" and "education" are often used interchangeably. However, *training* is best described as:

    a. skill-based instruction.

    b. knowledge-based instruction.

    c. increasing an understanding of concepts.

    d. preparation for future opportunities.

32. A primary attribute of training is that it produces:

    a. a highly formalized process.

    b. measurable performance outcomes.

    c. interdepartmental facilitation.

    d. individual characteristics consistent with company policy.

33. An organization wishes to provide training to improve employee morale. The first step in developing a training program is:

    a. designing a training plan.

    b. developing the curriculum.

    c. assessing the need for the training.

    d. hiring a certified trainer.

34. The training development process begins with which step?

    a. Performing a training needs analysis

    b. Ensuring that the budget has been approved

    c. Scheduling the training activities

    d. Developing the training materials

35. One of the primary benefits of performing a training needs analysis is:

    a. ensuring budget authority.

    b. demonstrating compliance with shareholder value.

    d. developing new supervisors and managers.

    d. providing management with objective evidence for training needs.

36. Which type of adult learner prefers traditional classroom training?

    a. Baby boomers

    b. Gen X

    c. Gen Y

    d. Gen Z

37. A type of training where a less experienced employee receives guidance from an experienced employee that may or may not be part of management is called:

    a. motivational.

    b. inspirational.

    c. self-directed.

    d. mentoring/coaching.

38. Which of the following methods would not be used to measure the effectiveness of a training program?

    a. Training certificate

    b. Observation

    c. Survey

    d. Pretesting and post-testing

39. Training that is based on the demonstration of measurable outcomes is _____ training.

    a. competency

    b. formal

    c. informal

    d. self-paced

40. This type of evaluation provides data about the effectiveness of a training program.

    a. Formative

    b. Summative

    c. Descriptive

    d. Affective

ANSWERS

1. b; Self-directed work teams are not affected by geography, time zones, staff schedules, and technology since members of this type of team are generally colocated and work the same shift. [III.A.1]

2. d; Team champions do not generally attend regular team meetings. [III.A.2]

3. d; Coaches work with the team leader and facilitator to move the team toward the objective and help provide resources for the completion of team member assignments. Additionally, they evaluate the team's progress. [III.A.2]

4. c; Good team members are characterized by actively participating in team meetings, communicating ideas and expertise, openly listening, and completing action assignments as scheduled. [III.A.3]

5. c; Cross-functional teams involve representation from various groups likely to be impacted by the changes. [III.A.1]

6. b; Without an understanding of how a team works and the individual behavior that advances team progress, the team will often get caught in personality concerns and turf wars. [III.A.4]

7. d; Formal teams have a specific goal or goals linked to the organization's plans. [III.A.1]

8. d; The team leader chairs team meetings and maintains team focus on the goal, and may in some cases be assisted by the facilitator. [III.A.2]

9. a; Coaches helps provide resources for completion of team member assignments. [III.A.2]

10. a; Virtual teams are made up of people in different locations who may never meet in person. Instead, the team may meet using teleconferencing facilities, or they may conduct all communication via e-mail. [III.A.1]

11. a; Team forming is when members struggle to understand the team goal and its meaning for them individually. [III.B.2]

12. c; Team norming is when members begin to understand the need to operate as a team rather than as a group of individuals. [III.B.2]

13. b; Team storming is when members express their own opinions and ideas, often disagreeing with others. [III.B.2]

14. a; Team performing is when team members work together to reach their common goal. [III.B.2]

15. b; Team forming is when members struggle to understand the team goal and its meaning for them individually. [III.B.2]

16. d; Individuals like to be recognized for their unique contributions. Some forms of recognition include the following:

    • Letters of appreciation sent to individuals and placed in personnel files

    • Public expressions of appreciation via meetings, newsletters, and so on

    • Positive feedback and comments from management

    • Inclusion in the performance appraisal

    [III.B.1]

17. d; Lack of adequate communication is one of the most frequently noted causes of team failure. [III.B.3]

18. d; Directional leadership is characterized by high directive and low supportive behavior. It is suited for individuals who possess low competence and high commitment. Such individuals are often described as the *enthusiastic beginner*. They are new to a task and motivated about it. [III.B.4]

19. b; Supportive leadership style is characterized by low directive and high supportive behavior. It is suited for individuals who possess mid competence and moderate commitment. Such individuals are often described as the *capable, but cautious, performer*. They know their task, but are not motivated about it. [III.B.4]

20. a; Delegative leadership style is characterized by low directive and low supportive behavior. It is suited for individuals who possess high competence and high commitment. Such individuals are often described as the *self-reliant achiever*. They are proficient in their task and are highly motivated about it. [III.B.4]

21. d; *Coaching* is a process by which a more experienced individual helps enhance the existing skills and capabilities that reside in a less experienced individual, while *mentoring* focuses on the individual from the career perspective. [III.C.1]

22. a; Consensus creates a situation or outcome that all the participants can live with. If no such situation or outcome can be found, discussion continues. [III.C.3]

23. c; Team ground rules and norms. The establishment of team norms is a helpful technique that is often initiated at the first team meeting. Team norms provide clear guidelines regarding what the team will and will not tolerate, and often define the consequences of violating the norms. [III.C.2]

24. a; Groupthink occurs within a group of people when the desire for harmony with other group members causes them to minimize conflict and reach consensus by actively suppressing dissenting viewpoints. [III.C.1]

25. b; The purpose of meetings is to generate ideas and solutions. [III.C.1]

26. b; Teams are generally better decision makers than individuals. [III.C.1]

27. d; Groupthink occurs within a group of people when the desire for harmony with other group members causes them to minimize conflict and reach consensus by actively suppressing dissenting viewpoints. [III.C.1]

28. c; Brainstorming is a group process used to generate ideas in a nonjudgmental way. The purpose of brainstorming is to generate a large number of ideas about an issue. [III.C.3]

29. a; Brainstorming is a group process used to generate ideas in a nonjudgmental way. The purpose of brainstorming is to generate a large number of ideas about an issue. [III.C.3]

30. d; Playing devil's advocate is a technique whereby by an individual opposes early consensus to generate further discussion and bring out other viewpoints. [III.C.1]

31. a; Education focuses on broadening an individual's knowledge base and expands thinking processes. Training is considered a subset of education that focuses on increasing proficiency in a skill. [III.D.1]

32. b; A primary attribute of training is that it produces measurable performance outcomes, whereas education alone does not. [III.D.1]

33. c; A training needs analysis is a diagnostic method used to identify the gap between current performance and desired performance. Organizational training needs stem from the strategic planning process, while individual training needs stem from both strategic planning and individual performance. [III.D.1]

34. a; A training needs analysis is a diagnostic method used to identify the gap between current performance and desired performance. Organizational training needs stem from the strategic planning process, while individual training needs stem from both strategic planning and individual performance. [III.D.1]

35. d; A training needs analysis effort produces facts about the target audience, training needs, learning styles, and so on. However, a good needs analysis does more than merely gather information. It makes a case for training. To that end, a training needs analysis must be well executed to garner top-down support. [III.D.1]

36. a; Baby boomers (born between 1946 and 1964) transfer learning to jobs, prefer formal classroom training, and have mixed feelings on computers and Internet use. [III.D.2]

37. d; Mentoring/coaching is used on a one-to-one basis to teach job-specific skills. [III.D.2]

38. a; Numerous methods exist for collecting data for evaluating training, including:

    • Follow-up survey and questionnaires

    • Observations on the job

    • Follow-up interviews

    • Follow-focus groups

    • Testing (pre- and post-training)

    • Performance monitoring

    • Review of operational data

    A training certificate does nothing more than verify attendance. [III.D.3]

39. a; Competency-based training is training that is based on measurable outcomes (proficiencies). [III.D.3]

40. b; Summative evaluations are completed at the end of training, whereas formative evaluations are usually administered at the midpoint. The purpose of these evaluations is to provide feedback on the instructor, training materials, and course environment. [III.D.3]

Part IV

Define

(40 questions)

A. VOICE OF THE CUSTOMER

1. *Customer identification.* Identify and segment customers and show how a project will impact both internal and external customers. (Apply)

2. *Customer data collection.* Identify and select appropriate data collection methods (e.g., surveys, focus groups, interviews, observations) to gather voice of the customer data. Ensure the data collection methods used are reviewed for validity and reliability. (Analyze)

3. *Customer requirements.* Define, select, and apply appropriate tools to determine customer needs and requirements, including critical-to-X (CTX when 'X' can be quality, cost, safety, etc.), CTQ tree, quality function deployment (QFD), supplier, input, process, output, customer (SIPOC) and Kano model. (Analyze)

B. BUSINESS CASE AND PROJECT CHARTER

1. *Business case.* Describe business case justification used to support projects. (Understand)

2. *Problem statement.* Develop a project problem statement and evaluate it in relation to baseline performance and improvement goals. (Evaluate)

3. *Project scope.* Develop and review project boundaries to ensure that the project has value to the customer. (Analyze)

4. *Goals and objectives.* Identify SMART (specific, measureable, actionable, relevant and time bound) goals and objectives on the basis of the project's problem statement and scope. (Analyze)

5. *Project performance measurements.* Identify and evaluate performance measurements (e.g., cost, revenue, delivery, schedule, customer satisfaction) that connect critical elements of the process to key outputs. (Analyze)

6. *Project charter review.* Explain the importance of having periodic project charter reviews with stakeholders. (Understand)

C. PROJECT MANAGEMENT (PM) TOOLS

Identify and use the following PM tools to track projects and document their progress. (Evaluate)

1. Gantt charts

2. Toll-gate reviews

3. Work breakdown structure (WBS)

4. RACI model (responsible, accountable, consulted and informed)

D. ANALYTICAL TOOLS

Identify and use the following analytical tools throughout the DMAIC cycle. (Apply)

1. Affinity diagrams

2. Tree diagrams

3. Matrix diagrams

4. Prioritization matrices

5. Activity network diagrams

QUESTIONS

1. *Specifications* most accurately represents:

    a. quality function deployment.

    b. critical-to-quality attributes.

    c. process limits.

    d. the voice of the customer.

Use the diagram below for questions 2–4.

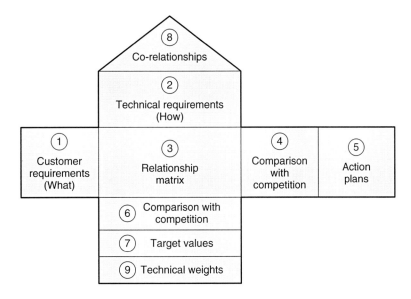

2. Which section shows whether the customer requirements will be met by the technical requirements?

    a. 3

    b. 6

    c. 4

    d. 1

3. Which section would show whether area 2 (technical requirements) has inverse related relationships?

    a. 3

    b. 8

    c. 6

    d. 4

4. Specifications would most likely be found in which section?

    a. 2

    b. 3

    c. 7

    d. 5

5. The X in *critical to X* stands for:

    a. any variable that impacts the customer.

    b. any constraints from production that need to be included in the design phase.

    c. quality.

    d. cost.

6. The tool that captures requirements on inputs into and outputs from a process is:

    a. quality function deployment.

    b. Kano model.

    c. requirements tree analysis.

    d. SIPOC.

7. QFD is an acronym for:

    a. quality function deployment.

    b. quality for design.

    c. quality forms development.

    d. quality through frequent delivery.

8. The voice of the customer is:

    a. the response heard from market promotions.

    b. an expression of customer wants.

    c. the communication method used for network marketing.

    d. a measure of capability of a process.

9. The house of quality is used to:

   a. organize a company into departments focusing on quality.

   b. structure the engineering team.

   c. translate customer needs into design specifications.

   d. calculate specifications for desired cost reductions.

10. In the Kano model, expected requirements are those that will cause:

    a. low customer dissatisfaction if not met, but high customer satisfaction if met.

    b. high customer dissatisfaction if not met, and high customer satisfaction if met.

    c. high customer dissatisfaction if not met, but low customer satisfaction if met.

    d. low customer dissatisfaction if not met, and low customer satisfaction if met.

For questions 11 and 12, use the paragraph below.

A quality engineer is requesting from management to dedicate one month out of the upcoming year to implementing quality initiatives that will reduce the defects seen at process A by 75%. These defects are 100% detectable at the next inspection step. The reduction in defects will save the company $7000 in the upcoming year.

11. Which of the following pieces of information is needed to develop the business case for implementing the project?

    a. Quality engineer's labor rate

    b. Type of defect

    c. Number of customer escapes

    d. Description of the quality initiative

12. Which of the following, if true, would make a good business case for the project?

    a. Quality engineer's salary < $84,000.

    b. The defect will be reduced by 100%.

    c. A poka-yoke is developed for the process.

    d. Management commitment to improving quality.

13. A good problem statement will:

    a. include the location of the issue.

    b. be qualitative.

    c. state the problem clearly and concisely.

    d. include potential root causes of the issue.

14. The project scope ensures that:

    a. the root cause is identified.

    b. the constraints of the project are clear.

    c. costs of the project are identified.

    d. the purpose of the project is clear.

15. A project is likely to fail if which of the following is true of the project scope?

    a. The scope is qualitative.

    b. The scope is too short.

    c. The scope is too long.

    d. The scope is too broad.

For questions 16 and 17, use the following paragraph.

> A quality engineer is requesting from management to dedicate one month out of the upcoming year to implementing a continuous improvement project that will increase the quality observed at process A from 70% to 96%. This initiative is in line with the organization's objective to maintain quality above 95%.

16. In terms of SMART goals, what is missing?

    a. Specific

    b. Measurable

    c. Realistic

    d. Time-bound

17. What makes the goal realistic?

    a. It only takes one month out of the year to complete.

    b. Quality will be increased from 70% to 96%.

    c. The goal is not realistic.

    d. The initiative is in line with the organization's objectives.

18. _____ helps manage the project by indicating the relative success of the project.

    a. Project performance measurement

    b. Project scope

    c. Project plan

    d. Project goals

19. According to Graham and Portny (2011), the three components of any project are scope, schedule, and:

    a. time.

    b. cost.

    c. quality.

    d. resources.

20. According to Williams (2008), the four components of any project are scope, quality, time, and:

    a. boundaries.

    b. schedule.

    c. constraints.

    d. cost.

21. The project management tool that allows you to see planned and completed tasks on a timeline is the:

    a. Gantt chart.

    b. affinity diagram.

    c. tree diagram.

    d. interrelationship diagram.

22. In a Gantt chart, task C cannot be completed until tasks A and B are completed. Tasks A and B would be considered:

    a. goals.

    b. predecessors.

    c. primary tasks.

    d. secondary tasks.

23. To ensure that all the activities for a particular stage in a process are completed before moving to the next stage, _____ are needed.

    a. tollgate reviews

    b. Gantt charts

    c. interrelationship diagrams

    d. work breakdown structures

24. When implementing a large project, the tool that should be used to show how the smaller activities are linked to larger activities is:

    a. tollgate reviews.

    b. Gantt charts.

    c. the interrelationship diagram.

    d. the work breakdown structure.

25. In a work breakdown structure, each time a larger activity is broken down into smaller activities, it is called a:

    a. phase.

    b. stage.

    c. level.

    d. grouping.

26. Work breakdown structures serve as inputs into tools such as the:

    a. affinity diagram.

    b. Gantt chart.

    c. FMEA.

    d. control plan.

27. In which role in the RACI model must the decision be discussed with the individual before a decision is made?

    a. Responsible

    b. Accountable

    c. Consulted

    d. Informed

28. In which role in the RACI model must the individual be cognizant about a decision because they are affected?

    a. Responsible

    b. Accountable

    c. Consulted

    d. Informed

29. In which role in the RACI model is the individual ultimately held responsible for results?

    a. Responsible

    b. Accountable

    c. Consulted

    d. Informed

30. In which role in the RACI model do the individuals actively participate in an activity?

    a. Responsible

    b. Accountable

    c. Consulted

    d. Informed

31. The tool that can be used to organize the ideas developed during a brainstorming session into larger categories is the:

    a. interrelationship diagram.

    b. Gantt chart.

    c. affinity diagram.

    d. work breakdown structure.

32. The affinity diagram is also known as the:

    a. interrelationship diagram.

    b. Gantt chart.

    c. work breakdown structure.

    d. KJ method.

33. In an affinity diagram, the themes into which the ideas are grouped:

    a. are coming from the ideas themselves.

    b. are predetermined.

    c. are generated in a separate brainstorming session on the categories.

    d. are determined by the organizer.

34. A tool used to show the activities and sub-activities necessary to complete a goal is the:

    a. tree diagram.

    b. interrelationship diagram.

    c. Gantt chart.

    d. work breakdown structure.

35. An organization chart is an example of a/an:

    a. interrelationship diagram.

    b. Gantt chart.

    c. work breakdown structure.

    d. tree diagram.

36. A tool that compares two or more sets of data to discover existing relationships is the:

    a. matrix diagram.

    b. affinity diagram.

    c. Gantt chart.

    d. work breakdown structure.

37. Quality function deployment is an example of a more complicated:

    a. affinity diagram.

    b. Gantt chart.

    c. work breakdown structure.

    d. matrix diagram.

38. A tool used to choose between several scenarios of unequal value is called a/an:

    a. prioritization matrix.

    b. relationship matrix.

    c. work breakdown structure.

    d. affinity diagram.

39. A tool used to show events occurring in a particular order or to demonstrate how events are connected is called a/an:

    a. activity network diagram.

    b. relationship matrix.

    c. work breakdown structure.

    d. prioritization matrix.

40. In an activity network diagram, the _____ determine(s) the minimal length of the entire project.

    a. levels

    b. critical path

    c. nodes

    d. slack times

ANSWERS

1. d; The QFD matrix helps illustrate the linkage between the VOC and the resulting technical requirements. [IV.A.3]

2. a; Area 3 is the relationship matrix. This area displays the strength of the relationship between the technical requirements and the customer requirements. [IV.A.3]

3. b; Area 8 displays co-relationships. This area shows the co-relationships between the technical requirements. A positive co-relationship indicates that both technical requirements can be improved at the same time. A negative co-relationship indicates that improving one of the technical requirements will worsen the other. [IV.A.3]

4. c; Area 7 contains the target values (specifications). This area contains a list of the target values for each of the technical requirements. [IV.A.3]

5. a; The concept behind critical to X (CtX), where X is a variable, is simply that X is an area or areas of impact on the customer. [IV.A.3]

6. d; A key benefit of the SIPOC is that it is much easier to complete than either a process map or a value stream map. SIPOCs can be used as a basis for constructing detailed process maps and value stream maps at future dates. Furthermore, SIPOCs help identify the voice of the customer as well as provide quick oversight into the initial X's and Y's. [IV.A.3]

7. a; Quality function deployment (QFD) provides a process for planning new or redesigned products and services. The input to the process is the voice of the customer (VOC). [IV.A.3]

8. b; Customers provide specifications for products or services explicitly; or customers express requirements in value terms—the components that influence the buy decision—such as price, product quality, innovation, service quality, company image, and reputation; or customers may spotlight only their needs or wants, thus leaving it up to the organization to translate them into internal specifications. [IV.A.1]

9. c; The QFD matrix, also known as the *house of quality*, helps illustrate the linkage between the VOC and the resulting technical requirements. [IV.A.3]

10. c; In the Kano model for customer satisfaction, requirements that will cause dissatisfaction if not present but will cause very little satisfaction if they are present are known as *expected requirements*. [IV.A.3]

11. a; A good business case will have a net profit. To calculate net profit, we need to know the revenue generated from the investment, and the investment cost.

To convert the investment cost into dollar units, we need to know the labor rate, which will be in terms of dollars/time.

Net profit = Revenue – Investment cost

Revenue = $7000

Investment cost = 1 month × QE labor rate

[IV.B.1]

12. a; A good business case will have a net profit. To calculate net profit, we need to know the revenue generated from the investment, and the investment cost. To convert the investment cost into dollar units, we need to know the labor rate, which will be in terms of dollars/time.

Net profit = Revenue – Investment cost

Revenue = $7000

Investment cost = 1 month × QE labor rate

For net profit to be positive, the QE salary would have to be < $84,000. [IV.B.1]

13. c; A good problem statement always needs to state the problem clearly and concisely to ensure that the subsequent root cause analysis is efficiently focusing on the problem. A good problem statement is not always qualitative, and is best when it is quantitative. Location is not always relevant in a problem statement. Root causes are not found in the problem statement. [IV.B.2]

14. b; The project scope ensures that resources are efficiently directed at solving a problem by placing clear constraints on the project. [IV.B.3]

15. d; The project scope ensures that resources are efficiently directed at solving a problem by placing clear constraints on the project. Making the scope too broad is in direct opposition to the essence of the project scope, and thus will always put the project or other projects in danger of failing. [IV.B.3]

16. d; SMART goals are:

S—Specific (Yes)

M—Measurable (70% to 96%)

A—Achievable (Not one of the choices)

R—Realistic (In line with company objectives)

T—Time-bound (Not defined)

The only part missing is when the goal will be completed. [IV.B.4]

17. d; A realistic goal is one that is in line with the organization's goals. [IV.B.4]

18. a; This is the definition of project performance measurements. Project performance measurements help to manage the project by indicating the relative success of the project. [IV.B.5]

19. d; According to Graham and Portny (2011), the three components of any project are scope, schedule, and resources. [IV.B.5]

20. d; According to Williams (2008), the four components of any project are scope, quality, time, and cost. [IV.B.5]

21. a; A Gantt chart is a type of bar chart used in process/project planning and control to display planned work and finished work in relation to time. It is also called a *milestone chart*. The Gantt chart provides an excellent visualization of time-based progress. [IV.C.1]

22. b; Predecessors are tasks that need to be completed before the next task can be completed. [IV.C.1]

23. a; Tollgate reviews ensure that all the tasks before the review are completed, and serve as a method of organization for a project. [IV.C.1]

24. d; The work breakdown structure is a tool that breaks down a project into smaller, manageable activities. [IV.C.1]

25. c; In a work breakdown structure, each time a larger activity is broken down into smaller activities, it is called a *level*. [IV.C.1]

26. b; Gantt charts use the outputs of a work breakdown structure to map out a project timeline. [IV.C.1]

27. c; RACI model (responsible, accountable, consulted, and informed). The RACI matrix is usually defined in detail by a team or committee, and in some cases, by an individual. The roles are:

    • Responsible—individuals who actively participate in an activity.

    • Accountable—the individual ultimately accountable for results. Only one individual may be accountable at a time.

    • Consulted—individuals who must be consulted before a decision is made.

    • Informed—individuals who must be informed about a decision because they are affected. These individuals do not need to take part in the decision-making process.

    [IV.C.1]

28. d; RACI model (responsible, accountable, consulted, and informed). The RACI matrix is usually defined in detail by a team or committee, and in some cases, by an individual. The roles are:

    • Responsible—individuals who actively participate in an activity.

    • Accountable—the individual ultimately accountable for results. Only one individual may be accountable at a time.

    • Consulted—individuals who must be consulted before a decision is made.

    • Informed—individuals who must be informed about a decision because they are affected. These individuals do not need to take part in the decision-making process.

    [IV.C.1]

29. b; RACI model (responsible, accountable, consulted, and informed). The RACI matrix is usually defined in detail by a team or committee, and in some cases, by an individual. The roles are:

    • Responsible—individuals who actively participate in an activity.

    • Accountable—the individual ultimately accountable for results. Only one individual may be accountable at a time.

    • Consulted—individuals who must be consulted before a decision is made.

    • Informed—individuals who must be informed about a decision because they are affected. These individuals do not need to take part in the decision-making process.

    [IV.C.1]

30. a; RACI model (responsible, accountable, consulted, and informed). The RACI matrix is usually defined in detail by a team or committee, and in some cases, by an individual. The roles are:

    • Responsible—individuals who actively participate in an activity.

    • Accountable—the individual ultimately accountable for results. Only one individual may be accountable at a time.

    • Consulted—individuals who must be consulted before a decision is made.

    • Informed—individuals who must be informed about a decision because they are affected. These individuals do not need to take part in the decision-making process.

    [IV.C.1]

Part IV
Answers

31. c; The affinity diagram is a tool used to organize information and help achieve order out of the chaos that can develop in a brainstorming session. Large amounts of data, concepts, and ideas are grouped based on their natural relationships to one another. [IV.D]

32. d; The affinity diagram is also known as the *KJ method.* [IV.D]

33. a; Without talking, participants look for related ideas and gather them into logical groups. Also, participants may move notes that other participants have moved. If notes appear to belong to more than one group, replicate a note for each group. It is OK to have outliers or lone ideas. [IV.D]

34. a; The tree diagram is a tool that depicts the hierarchy of tasks and subtasks needed to complete an objective. The finished diagram resembles a tree. Tree diagrams may be depicted either vertically top-down or horizontally left-to-right. When depicted top-down, tasks move from general (top) to specific (down), and when depicted left-to-right, tasks move from general (left) to specific (right). [IV.D]

35. d; Tree diagrams may be used in a wide variety of situations, including a critical-to-quality tree, decision tree, fault tree analysis, Gozinto chart, organization chart, process decision program chart, five whys, work breakdown structure (WBS), and so on. [IV.D]

36. a; The matrix diagram is a tool that identifies the relationships that exist between groups of data. It can also be used to identify the strength of those relationships. The matrix diagram does not use a singular format. Instead, there are six different forms, including the C, L, T, X, Y, and roof-shaped formats. [IV.D]

37. d; The roof-shaped matrix is used with an L- or T-shaped matrix to show one group of items relating to itself. It is most commonly used with a house of quality, where it forms the "roof" of the "house." [IV.D]

38. a; The prioritization matrix is a tool used to choose between several options that have many useful benefits, but where not all of them are of equal value. The choices are prioritized according to known weighted criteria and then narrowed down to the most desirable or effective one(s) to accomplish the task or problem at hand. [IV.D]

39. a; The activity network diagram (AND) is a tool used to illustrate a sequence of events or activities (nodes) and the interconnectivity of such nodes. It is used for scheduling, and especially for determining the critical path through nodes. It is also known as an *arrow diagram.* [IV.D]

40. b; The critical path is the path from start to finish that requires the most time. [IV.D]

Part V

Measure

(88 questions)

A. PROCESS CHARACTERISTICS

1. *Process flow metrics.* Identify and use process flow metrics (e.g., work in progress (WIP), work in queue (WIQ), touch time, takt time, cycle time, throughput) to determine constraints. Describe the impact that "hidden factories" can have on process flow metrics. (Analyze)

2. *Process analysis tools.* Select, use and evaluate various tools, e.g., value stream maps, process maps, work instructions, flowcharts, spaghetti diagrams, circle diagrams, gemba walk. (Evaluate)

B. DATA COLLECTION

1. *Types of data.* Define, classify, and distinguish between qualitative and quantitative data, and continuous and discrete data. (Evaluate)

2. *Measurement scales.* Define and use nominal, ordinal, interval, and ratio measurement scales. (Apply)

3. *Sampling.* Define and describe sampling concepts, including representative selection, homogeneity, bias, accuracy, and precision. Determine the appropriate sampling method (e.g., random, stratified, systematic, subgroup, block) to obtain valid representation in various situations. (Evaluate)

4. *Data collection plans and methods.* Develop and implement data collection plans that include data capture and processing tools, e.g., check sheets, data coding, data cleaning (imputation techniques). Avoid data collection pitfalls by defining the metrics to be used or collected, ensuring that collectors are trained in the tools and understand how the data will be used, and checking for seasonality effects. (Analyze)

C. MEASUREMENT SYSTEMS

1. *Measurement system analysis (MSA).* Use gauge repeatability and reproducibility (R&R) studies and other MSA tools (e.g., bias, correlation, linearity, precision to tolerance, percent agreement) to analyze measurement system capability. (Evaluate)

2. *Measurement systems across the organization.* Identify how measurement systems can be applied to marketing, sales, engineering, research and development (R&D), supply chain management, and customer satisfaction data. (Understand)

3. *Metrology.* Define and describe elements of metrology, including calibration systems, traceability to reference standards, and the control and integrity of measurement devices and standards. (Understand)

D. BASIC STATISTICS

1. *Basic statistical terms.* Define and distinguish between population parameters and sample statistics, e.g., proportion, mean, standard deviation. (Apply)

2. *Central limit theorem.* Explain the central limit theorem and its significance in the application of inferential statistics for confidence intervals, hypothesis tests, and control charts. (Understand)

3. *Descriptive statistics.* Calculate and interpret measures of dispersion and central tendency. (Evaluate)

4. *Graphical methods.* Construct and interpret diagrams and charts, e.g., box-and-whisker plots, scatter diagrams, histograms, normal probability plots, frequency distributions, cumulative frequency distributions. (Evaluate)

5. *Valid statistical conclusions.* Distinguish between descriptive and inferential statistical studies. Evaluate how the results of statistical studies are used to draw valid conclusions. (Evaluate)

E. PROBABILITY

1. *Basic concepts.* Describe and apply probability concepts, e.g., independence, mutually exclusive events, addition and multiplication rules, conditional probability, complementary probability, joint occurrence of events. (Apply)

2. *Distributions.* Describe, interpret, and use various distributions, e.g., normal, Poisson, binomial, chi square, Student's t, F, hypergeometric, bivariate, exponential, lognormal, Weibull. (Evaluate)

F. PROCESS CAPABILITY

1. *Process capability indices.* Define, select, and calculate C_p and C_{pk}. (Evaluate)

2. *Process performance indices.* Define, select, and calculate P_p, P_{pk}, C_{pm}, and process sigma. (Evaluate)

3. *General process capability studies.* Describe and apply elements of designing and conducting process capability studies relative to characteristics, specifications, sampling plans, stability and normality. (Evaluate)

4. *Process capability for attributes data.* Calculate the process capability and process sigma level for attributes data. (Apply)

5. *Process capability for non-normal data.* Identify non-normal data and determine when it is appropriate to use Box-Cox or other transformation techniques. (Apply)

6. *Process performance vs. specification.* Distinguish between natural process limits and specification limits. Calculate process performance metrics, e.g., percent defective, parts per million (PPM), defects per million opportunities (DPMO), defects per unit (DPU), throughput yield, rolled throughput yield (RTY). (Evaluate)

7. *Short-term and long-term capability.* Describe and use appropriate assumptions and conventions when only short-term data or only long-term data are available. Interpret the relationship between short-term and long-term capability. (Evaluate)

QUESTIONS

1. The material that has been input into the process, but that has not reached the output or finished stage can be defined as:

   a. touch time.

   b. takt time.

   c. work in progress (WIP).

   d. work in queue (WIQ).

2. The material waiting to be processed is defined as:

   a. work in queue (WIQ).

   b   work in progress (WIP).

   c. touch time.

   d. takt time.

3. The time that a unit of product is being worked on at any step in the process is defined as:

   a. work in queue (WIQ).

   b. work in progress (WIP).

   c. touch time.

   d. takt time.

4. The time required to complete one unit from the beginning of the process to the end of the process is defined as:

   a. touch time.

   b. cycle time.

   c. takt time.

   d. throughput.

5. The rate in time per unit at which the process must complete units in order to achieve the customer demand is defined as:

   a. touch time.

   b. cycle time.

   c. takt time.

   d. throughput.

6. The amount of output that passes through the process in a specified period of time is defined as:

   a. touch time.

   b. cycle time.

   c. takt time.

   d. throughput.

7. The customer demand stated in units per time is the:

   a. cycle time.

   b. takt time.

   c. takt rate.

   d. throughput.

8. A customer requires 116 units per day. The plant operates one eight-hour shift. What is the required takt time?

   a. 116

   b. 14.5

   c. 8

   d. 4.14

9. A customer requires 116 units per day. The plant operates one eight-hour shift. What is the required takt rate?

   a. 0.13

   b. 0.24

   c. 0.48

   d. 116

10. When a process changes the form, fit, or function of a product, this is referred to as:

    a. work in queue (WIQ).

    b. work in progress (WIP).

    c. touch time.

    d. value-added activity.

11. The time from the last unit on one job to the first good unit of the next job is referred as the:

    a. changeover time.

    b. cycle time.

    c. takt time.

    d. takt rate.

12. Which of the following is considered to be qualitative data?

    a. kilo

    b. meter

    c. liter

    d. color

13. This type of data is classified into categories with no order implied.

    a. Ordinal

    b. Interval

    c. Ratio

    d. Nominal

14. This type of data positions data in a series, where order is important, but precise differences between values aren't defined.

    a. Interval

    b. Ratio

    c. Ordinal

    d. Nominal

15. This type of data has meaningful differences but no absolute zero, so ratios aren't useful.

    a. Ratio

    b. Ordinal

    c. Nominal

    d. Interval

16. This type of data has meaningful differences, and an absolute zero exists.

    a. Interval

    b. Ratio

    c. Ordinal

    d. Nominal

17. Which of the following is not considered continuous data?

    a. The number of defects per unit

    b. The weight of a raw material

    c. The output voltage of a transformer

    d. The cycle time for a filling operation

18. An injection molding process has a four-cavity mold running in one press. What sampling method is most appropriate to monitor this process?

    a. Double sampling

    b. Simple random sampling

    c. Stratified sampling

    d. Multiple sampling

19. A powder coating operation is being monitored. Which of the following is not considered discrete data?

    a. Go/no-go measurements

    b. Errors in the batch record

    c. Pass/fail color sheen test

    d. Number of nonconforming parts

20. Which measurement scale should be used to measure customer satisfaction using the Likert response scale?

    a. Nominal

    b. Ordinal

    c. Interval

    d. Ratio

21. Which of the following components of a measurement system is associated with different operators and different gages?

    a. Stability

    b. Linearity

    c. Bias

    d. Reproducibility

22. If the bias of a measuring system increases across the measurement range, the measuring device is said to have poor:

    a. stability.

    b. linearity.

    c. bias.

    d. reproducibility.

Use the following figure to answer questions 23 and 24.

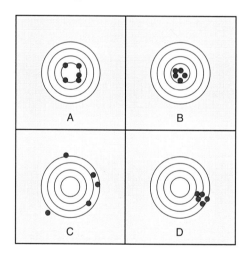

23. Which of the targets indicates good repeatability but poor bias?

    a. A

    b. B

    c. C

    d. D

24. Which of the targets indicates good repeatability, bias, and linearity?

    a. A

    b. B

    c. C

    d. D

25. Calculate the precision-to-tolerance ratio (PTR) using the flowing information:

    Lower specification limit –150

    Upper specification limit 150

    σ_{MS} 8.45

    a. 16.9%

    b. 28.1%

    c. 32.7%

    d. 41.3%

26. A measurement system has been evaluated with the following results: repeatability 0.13% and reproducibility 10.38%. What is the gage R&R?

    a. 0.13%

    b. 1.35%

    c. 10.25%

    d. 10.38%

27. If a gage R&R study is conducted with three inspection technicians, how many degrees of freedom (df) are available for the inspectors?

    a. 1

    b. 2

    c. 3

    d. 4

28. Which of the following is considered to be a type A uncertainty in a gage R&R?

    a. Physical constants

    b. Environmental effects

c. Manufacturer's specification

d. Stability

29. Which of the following is considered to be a type B uncertainty in a gage R&R?

   a. Reference standards

   b. Repeatability

   c. Linearity

   d. Bias

30. The distribution of sample averages will tend toward a normal distribution as the sample size, n, approaches infinity. This phenomenon is referred to as the:

   a. Gaussian statistics.

   b. central limit theorem.

   c. exponential distribution.

   d. kappa statistic.

31. For the normal curve, approximately 68% of the data will fall between:

   a. $\pm 1\sigma$

   b. $\pm 2\sigma$

   c. $\pm 3\sigma$

   d. $\pm 5\sigma$

32. The type of frequency distribution that is most commonly found in quality work is the:

   a. hypergeometric.

   b. uniform.

   c. normal.

   d. binomial.

33. The peakedness of the data is called:

   a. kurtosis.

   b. skewness.

   c. leptosis.

   d. modal.

34. The lack of symmetry of the data is called:

    a. kurtosis.

    b. leptosis.

    c. skewness.

    d. modality.

35. Which of the following can be used to demonstrate normality?

    a. Histograms

    b. Probability plots

    c. Chi-square goodness-of-fit test

    d. All of these tests are appropriate to demonstrate normality

36. A scatter diagram:

    a. compares two variables.

    b. orders data from highest to lowest.

    c. has causes such as materials, methods, and measurements.

    d. only indicates linear relationships.

37. Given the sample set of data 45, 51, 46, 53, 46, 57, 51, 72, 55, 61, calculate the mean.

    a. 52.00

    b. 53.70

    c. 55.60

    d. 57.12

38. Given the sample set of data 45, 51, 46, 53, 46, 57, 51, 72, 55, 61, calculate the variance.

    a. 2.15

    b. 8.23

    c. 53.70

    d. 67.79

39. A variable is:

    a. a measurable quality characteristic.

    b. a "good/bad" type characteristic.

c. synonymous with *attribute*.

d. always discrete.

40. When a quick measure of dispersion is desired, use the:

    a. variance.

    b. standard deviation.

    c. range.

    d. median.

41. The center value of a cell in a frequency distribution for grouped data is called the:

    a. boundary.

    b. midpoint.

    c. interval.

    d. tally.

42. Variables data that have gaps are called:

    a. measurable.

    b. probability.

    c. discrete.

    d. continuous.

43. When an accurate measure of the dispersion is desired, use the:

    a. standard error.

    b. mean deviation.

    c. standard deviation.

    d. mode.

44. Given the sample set of data 45, 51, 46, 53, 57, calculate the median.

    a. 51.00

    b. 53.70

    c. 55.60

    d. 57.12

45. Given the sample set of data 43, 45, 40, 39, 42, 44, 41, calculate the sample variance.

    a. 2.15

    b. 4.67

    c. 53.70

    d. 67.79

46. Given the sample set of data 43, 45, 40, 39, 42, 44, 41, calculate the kurtosis.

    a. 1.23

    b. 1.50

    c. 2.60

    d. 8.23

47. Given the sample set of data 43, 45, 40, 39, 42, 44, 41, calculate the skewness.

    a. 0.00

    b. 1.74

    c. 2.60

    d. 0.23

48. Given the sample set of data 43, 45, 40, 39, 42, 44, 41, calculate the standard error.

    a. 1.23

    b. 1.54

    c. 1.77

    d. 8.23

49. A process has a mean of 53.7 and sigma of 8.23. What percentage of product generated will be greater than 60?

    a. 22%

    b. 25%

    c. 75%

    d. 78%

50. A process has a mean of 53.7 and sigma of 8.23. What percentage of product generated will be less than 40?

a. 1%

b. 5%

c. 95%

d. 98%

51. A process has a mean of 53.7 and sigma of 8.23. What value (x) for the upper specification limit will yield 5% scrap?

a. 47

b. 57

c. 67

d. 77

52. A process has a mean of 53.7 and sigma of 8.23. What value (x) for the lower specification limit will yield 5% scrap?

a. 30

b. 40

c. 50

d. 60

53. When the word "and" is verbalized in probability, it means to perform the arithmetic operation of:

a. multiplication.

b. addition.

c. division.

d. exponentiation.

54. The parenthesis value in the Poisson table is:

a. an exact value.

b. a natural number.

c. a cumulative value.

d. not needed.

55. Which of the following is a method of counting events?

a. Addition

b. Outcomes

c. Division

d. Permutation

56. The probability of two or less is equal to:

a. P0 + P1.

b. (P0) (P1) (P2).

c. P0 + P1 + P2.

d. (P0) (P1).

57. When the word "or" is verbalized in probability, it means to perform the arithmetic operation of:

a. multiplication.

b. division.

c. addition.

d. exponentiation.

58. When the occurrence of one event negates the possibility of another event, it is called:

a. independent.

b. mutually exclusive.

c. dependent.

d. mutually inclusive.

59. The type of frequency distribution that is used for finite discrete data is the:

a. hypergeometric.

b. uniform.

c. normal.

d. binomial.

60. The multiplicative theorem is concerned with:

a. independent events.

b. mutually exclusive events.

c. dependent events.

d. event frequency.

61. When the occurrence of an event has no influence on the occurrence of a second event, it is called:

a. independent.

b. mutually inclusive.

c. mutually exclusive.

d. dependent.

62. Which of the following is a method of counting events?

a. Addition

b. Outcomes

c. Division

d. Combination

63. What is the main difference between a permutation and a combination?

a. The number of combinations is generally larger than the number of permutations.

b. Order is important in a combination, but not a permutation.

c. Order is important in a permutation, but not a combination.

d. A permutation only applies to a large number of items.

64. What type of diagrams can be used to graphically display probability?

a. Fishbone

b. Flow

c. Venn

d. Pareto

65. Which of the following distributions is used for continuous data?

a. Hypergeometric

    b. Binomial

    c. Poisson

    d. Normal

66. If something has a "fifty-fifty chance" of occurring, what is the probability that it will occur?

    a. 1

    b. 5

    c. 0.5

    d. 50

67. As parts are made, they are placed in trays that hold 30 parts. If a tray contains six defective parts and you sample one part from the tray, what is the probability that it will be a defective part?

    a. 6%

    b. 20%

    c. 30%

    d. 80%

68. A newly formed ASQ Section consists of 12 members. How many slates (permutations) of officers could be formed if the offices of chair, vice chair, and secretary are filled?

    a. 4

    b. 12

    c. 220

    d. 1320

69. A project team consists of 12 members. How many subcommittees of three could be formed?

    a. 4

    b. 12

    c. 220

    d. 1320

70. A coil of steel has an overage of five nonconformances. What is the probability of three nonconformances in a randomly selected coil?

a. 3%

b. 5%

c. 14%

d. 22%

71. If there are five different parts to be stocked, but only three bins available, what is the number of permutations of the five parts in the three bins?

a. 3

b. 5

c. 15

d. 60

72. A sample of three numbers is selected from the numbers 1 to 45. How many different combinations are possible?

a. 14,190

b. 28,380

c. 42,570

d. 85,140

73. An inspector samples four circuit boards from a steady stream of circuit boards that is known to be 12% nonconforming. What is the probability of selecting two nonconforming units in the sample?

a. 0

b. 0.067

c. 0.12

d. 0.5

74. An inspector randomly selects three parts from a lot of 20 that is known to be 10% nonconforming. What is the probability that the selected samples will contain no nonconforming units?

a. 0

b. 0.5

c. 0.716

d. 1

75. Which of the following cases would be considered the most desirable in terms of the relationship of the specification to the process spread?

    a. $6\sigma < USL - LSL$

    b. $6\sigma > USL - LSL$

    c. $6\sigma = USL - LSL$

    d. $3\sigma = USL$

76. Of the following, which capability index is the most desirable?

    a. 1.00

    b. 1.50

    c. 0.75

    d. 0.30

77. Which of the following cases would be considered the least desirable in terms of the relationship of the specification to the process spread?

    a. $6\sigma < USL - LSL$

    b. $6\sigma = USL - LSL$

    c. $6\sigma > USL - LSL$

    d. $3\sigma = USL$

78. The process spread is the same as the:

    a. tolerance.

    b. quality spread.

    c. index.

    d. process variation.

79. The numerator of the capability index equation is the:

    a. tolerance.

    b. capability ratio.

    c. process spread.

    d. standard error.

80. Given the following information, calculate the C_r capability ratio: $\bar{\bar{X}}$ 904.573, $\bar{R}$ 36.933, n 5, s 15.85, target 900, lower specification limit 850, upper specification limit 950.

    a. 0.951

    b. 1.051

    c. 2.315

    d. 2.798

81. Given the following information, calculate the C_p capability index: $\bar{\bar{X}}$ 904.573, $\bar{R}$ 36.933, n 5, s 15.85, target 900, lower specification limit 850, upper specification limit 950.

    a. 0.951

    b. 1.052

    c. 2.315

    d. 2.798

82. Given the following information, calculate the C_{pk} process capability ratio: $\bar{\bar{X}}$ 904.573, $\bar{R}$ 36.933, n 5, s 15.85, target 900, lower specification limit 850, upper specification limit 950.

    a. 0.375

    b. 0.567

    c. 0.955

    d. 1.147

83. What is the process capability on an attributes control chart?

    a. The same as a variables control chart

    b. Plus or minus half of the control limits

    c. The process average

    d. None of these

84. What can you tell about a process if $C_{pk} = 0.85$ and $C_p = 1.1$?

    a. The process is capable and centered within the specification limits.

    b. The process is centered within the specification limits, but is not capable.

   c. The process is not centered and not capable.

   d. The process is narrow enough to be capable, but is not centered.

85. Given the following information for a *p*-chart, calculate the process capability: sum of *np* 55, sum *n* 2800, *n* 200.

   a. 0

   b. 0.020

   c. 0.125

   d. Not enough information provided to calculate

86. Given the following information for an *np*-chart, calculate the process capability: sum of *np* 55, *k* 14, *n* 200.

   a. 0

   b. 0.020

   c. 3.929

   d. 4.133

87. Given the following information for a *c*-chart, calculate the process capability: sum of *c* 37, *k* 14.

   a. 0

   b. 2.643

   c. 3.259

   d. 4.133

88. Given the following information for a *u*-chart, calculate the process capability: sum of *c* 244, sum of *n* 112, *n* 6.

   a. 0

   b. 2.179

   c. 3.986

   d. 4.133

ANSWERS

1. c; Work in progress (WIP) is the material that has been input into the process, but that has not reached the output or finished stage. This includes the material being processed, waiting to be processed, or stored as inventory at each step. [V.A.1]

2. a; Work in queue (WIQ) is the material waiting to be processed by one or more steps in the process and is one component of WIP. [V.A.1]

3. c; Touch time is the time that a unit of product is being worked on at any step in the process. [V.A.1]

4. b; Cycle time is the time required to complete one unit from the beginning of the process to the end of the process. [V.A.1]

5. c; Takt time is the rate in time per unit at which the process must complete units to achieve the customer demand. [V.A.1]

6. d; Throughput is the amount of output that passes through the process in a specified period. [V.A.1]

7. c; Takt time (the reciprocal of the takt rate) is the customer demand stated in units per time. [V.A.1]

8. d;

$$\text{Takt time} = \frac{\text{Time available}}{\text{Number of units to be produced}} = \frac{8 \times 60}{116}$$

$$= 4.14 \text{ minutes per unit}$$

[V.A.1]

9. b;

$$\text{Takt rate} = \frac{\text{Number of units to be produced}}{\text{Time available}} = \frac{116}{8 \times 60}$$

$$= 0.24 \text{ units per minutes}$$

[V.A.1]

10. d; Value-added activity is any activity that adds value to a product or service. In the case of a product, the value-added work changes the form, fit, or function of a product. [V.A.1]

11. a; Changeover time is the time from the last unit on one job to the first good unit of the next job, and includes the time it takes to remove all the dies and tooling from the previous job and replace them with the dies and tooling for the next job. [V.A.1]

12. d; Qualitative data are data based on descriptive information rather than numerical information. [V.B.1]

13. d; Nominal scales classify data into categories with no order implied. [V.B.2]

14. c; Ordinal scales refer to positions in a series, where order is important but precise differences between values aren't defined. [V.B.2]

15. d; Interval scales have meaningful differences but no absolute zero, so ratios aren't useful. [V.B.2]

16. b; Ratio scales have meaningful differences, and an absolute zero exists. [V.B.2]

17. a; Discrete data are count data, and are sometimes called *categorical* or *attribute* data. [V.B.1]

18. c; When a population can be divided naturally into groups, it is best to use stratified sampling techniques. [V.B.3]

19. c; Although the test result is recorded as pass/fail, the measurement itself is on a continuous scale. [V.B.3]

20. b; Rating of a service is classified into categories where order is important. The precise difference between values is not defined. [V.B.3]

21. d; Reproducibility is the precision under conditions where independent measurement results are obtained with the same method on identical measurement items with different operators using different equipment. [V.C.1]

22. b; Linearity is the difference in bias through the operating range of measurements. A measurement system that has good linearity will have a constant bias no matter the magnitude of measurement. [V.C.1]

23. d; This grouping shows good repeatability (precision), and linearity, but low accuracy due to bias. [V.C.1]

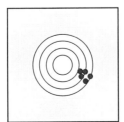

24. b; This grouping shows good repeatability (precision), linearity, bias, and accuracy. [V.C.1]

25. a;

$$\text{PTR} = \frac{6\hat{\sigma}_{ms}}{\text{USL} - \text{LSL}} = \frac{6 \times 8.45}{150 - (-150)} = 0.169 \text{ or } 16.9\%$$

[V.C.1]

26. d;

$$\text{GRR} = \sqrt{EV^2 + AV^2} = \sqrt{0.132^2 + 10.38^2} = 10.38\%$$

[V.C.1]

27. b;

$$\text{df}_{\text{Appraisers}} = r - 1 = 3 - 1 = 2$$

where

r = Number of inspectors (appraisers)

When using three inspectors, there are 2 degrees of freedom available.

[V.C.1]

28. d; Type A uncertainties are those that can be calculated by statistical means, such as repeatability, reproducibility, accuracy, linearity, bias, and stability. [V.C.1]

29. a; Type B uncertainties are uncertainties associated with measurement systems that cannot be evaluated by statistical methods. Type B uncertainty is typically established by previous experience and does not rely on statistical calculations, or simply, is any uncertainty that is not type A. [V.C.1]

30. b; The central limit theorem states that the distribution of sample averages will tend toward a normal distribution as the sample size, n, approaches infinity. [V.D.2]

31. a; The percentages for ±1, 2, and 3 standard deviations are provided in the figure. [V.D.1]

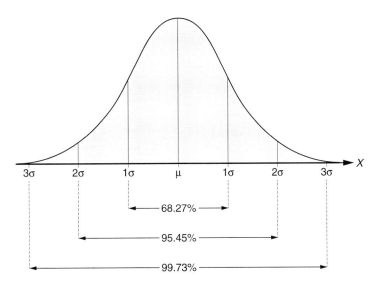

32. c; The normal distribution is the most widely used distribution. It is the basis for the $\bar{X}$ and R chart. [V.D.1]

33. a; Kurtosis measures the degree to which a set of data is peaked or flat. [V.D.1]

34. c; Skewness measures the degree to which a set of data is not symmetrical. [V.D.1]

35. d; Normality can be assessed by analytical and graphical methods. Histograms, probability plots, and chi-square goodness-of-fit tests are three commonly used methods used to test for normality. [V.D.4]

36. a; A scatter diagram is a plot of two variables, one on the y-axis and the other on the axis. The resulting graph allows visual examination for patterns to determine whether the variables show a relationship. [V.D.4]

37. b; The mean for the sample set of data 45, 51, 46, 53, 46, 57, 51, 72, 55, 61 is 53.7.

    This is an easy calculation using a simple scientific calculator. [V.D.3]

38. d; The variance for the sample set of data 45, 51, 46, 53, 46, 57, 51, 72, 55, 61 is 67.79.

    This is an easy calculation using a simple scientific calculator. Ensure the $n - 1$ option is used because the data set is a sample. Typically, the calculator will give the standard deviation, which is then squared to obtain the variance. [V.D.3]

Part V
Answers

39. a; Basically, there are two types of data to collect as a part of a problem-solving process: attribute data, or go/no-go information, and variable data, or measurement information. [V.D.1]

40. c; The range is simply the highest value minus the lowest value. It is the easiest measurement of dispersion to calculate. [V.D.3]

41. b; The midpoint of a cell in a frequency distribution for grouped data is the value in the center, and the most representative value within the cell. [V.D.3]

42. c; When variable data can take on any value between two specified values, it is called a *continuous variable*; otherwise, it is called a *discrete variable*. [V.B.1]

43. c; Standard deviation is the computed measure of variability indicating the spread of the data set around the mean. The range is simply the lowest value subtracted from the highest value and does not yield as much information. [V.D.3]

44. a; The median is simply the value in the middle in an ordered set of numbers. In this case, 45, 46, 51, 53, 57. [V.D.3]

45. b; To calculate the sample variance for the sample set of data 43, 45, 40, 39, 42, 44, 41, use the following formula:

$$s^2 = \frac{\Sigma\left(X - \bar{X}\right)^2}{n-1}$$

where

$\bar{X}$ = Sample mean

X = Data point

n = The number of data points in the sample

$$s^2 = \frac{\Sigma\left(X - \bar{X}\right)^2}{n-1} = \frac{28}{7-1} = 4.67$$

This is a simple calculation on a scientific calculator.

46. b; To calculate the kurtosis for the sample set of data 43, 45, 40, 39, 42, 44, 41, use the following formula:

$$\text{Kurtosis} = \frac{\Sigma x\left(X - \bar{X}\right)^4}{\left(n-1\right)s^4}$$

where

$\bar{X}$ = Sample mean

s = Sample standard deviation

X = Data point

n = The number of data points in the sample

$$\text{Kurtosis} = \frac{\Sigma x \left(X - \bar{X} \right)^4}{(n-1)s^4} = \frac{196}{(7-1) \times 2.16^4} = 1.50$$

[V.D.3]

47. a; To calculate the skewness for the sample set of data 43, 45, 40, 39, 42, 44, 41, use the following formula:

$$\text{Skewness} = \frac{\Sigma x \left(X - \bar{X} \right)^3}{(n-1)s^3}$$

where:

$\bar{X}$ = Sample mean

s = Sample standard deviation

X = Data point

n = The number of data points in the sample

$$\text{Skewness} = \frac{\Sigma x \left(X - \bar{X} \right)^3}{(n-1)s^3} = \frac{0}{(7-1) \times 2.16^3} = 0.00$$

[V.D.3]

48. c; To calculate the standard error for the sample set of data 43, 45, 40, 39, 42, 44, 41, use the following formula:

$$s_{\bar{x}} = \frac{s}{\sqrt{n}} = \frac{2.15}{\sqrt{7}} = 0.82$$

Note: The standard deviation is 4.67 and the sample size is 7. [V.D.3]

49. a; For any data set that is normally distributed and for which the mean and the standard deviation are known or can be estimated, the probability of falling above or below any standard normal values or z-scores can be calculated using the following formula:

$$z = \frac{x - \mu}{\sigma}$$

For a process with a mean of 53.7 and sigma of 8.23, what percentage of product generated will be greater than 60?

$$z = \frac{60 - 53.7}{8.23} = 0.765$$

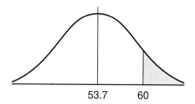

Looking up *z*-value 0.765 in Appendix B, Normal Distribution Probability Points—Area above Z from Durivage (2014) indicates that approximately 22% of product produced will be greater than 60. [V.E.2]

50. b; For any data set that is normally distributed and for which the mean and the standard deviation are known or can be estimated, the probability of falling above or below any standard normal values or *z*-scores can be calculated using the following formula:

$$z = \frac{x - \mu}{\sigma}$$

For a process with a mean of 53.7 and sigma of 8.23, what percentage of product generated will be less than 40?

$$z = \frac{40 - 53.7}{8.23} = -1.665$$

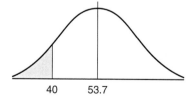

Looking up *z*-value 1.665 (note that the minus sign can be dropped) in Appendix B, Normal Distribution Probability Points—Area above Z from Durivage (2014) indicates that approximately 5% of product produced will be less than 40. [V.E.2]

51. c; For a process with a mean of 53.7 and sigma of 8.23, the value (*x*) for the upper specification limit that will yield 5% scrap can be calculated by

$$x = \mu + z\sigma$$

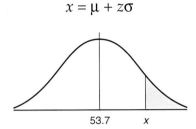

53.7   *x*

Looking up the *z*-value that yields approximately 5% in Appendix B, Normal Distribution Probability Points—Area above Z from Durivage (2014) shows that the *z*-value is approximately 1.65.

$$x = 53.7 + 1.65 \times 8.23 = 67$$

An upper value of 67 will yield approximately 5% scrap. [V.E.2]

52. b; For a process with a mean of 53.7 and sigma of 8.23, the value (*x*) for the lower specification limit that will yield 5% scrap can be calculated by

$$x = \mu - z\sigma$$

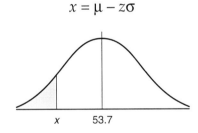

x   53.7

Looking up *z*-value 1.665 (note that the minus sign can be dropped) in Appendix B, Normal Distribution Probability Points—Area above Z from Durivage (2014) shows that the *z*-value is approximately 1.65.

$$x = 53.7 - 1.65 \times 8.23 = 40$$

A lower value of 40 will yield approximately 5% scrap. [V.E.2]

53. a; Probability theorem 6. If A and B are independent events (one where its occurrence has no influence on the probability of the other event or events), then the probability of both A and B occurring is the product of their respective probabilities: P(A and B) = P(A) × P(B). In other words, whenever an "and" is verbalized, the mathematical operation is multiplication. [V.E.1]

54. c; When present, cumulative values are contained in parentheses in Poisson tables. Some references will provide a separate table of cumulative values. The user should be certain of the values the table is providing. [V.E.2]

55. d; A permutation is a counting technique that requires an ordered arrangement of a set of objects:

$$P(n,k) = \frac{n!}{(n-k)!}$$

where there are n items and we want to find the number of ways k items can be ordered. [V.E.1]

56. c; The probability of two or less is equal to P0 + P1 + P2. This comes from probability theorem 5: the sum of the probabilities of events of a situation is equal to 1.0. [V.E.1]

57. c; Whenever "or" is verbalized, the mathematical operation is addition. Refer to probability theorems 3 and 4.

    Theorem 3. If A and B are two mutually exclusive events (the occurrence of one event makes the other event impossible), then the probability that either event A or event B will occur is the sum of their respective probabilities: P(A or B) = P(A) + P(B).

    Theorem 4. If event A and event B are not mutually exclusive, then the probability of either event A or event B or both is given by P(A or B or both) = P(A) + P(B) – P(both). [V.E.1]

58. c; A dependent event is one whose occurrence influences the probability of the other event or events. [V.E.1]

59. a; The hypergeometric distribution, which is used for finite discrete data when the random sample taken is not replaced. The formula is constructed of three combinations (total, nonconforming, and conforming).

$$P(x) = \frac{C_{n-x}^{N-M} C_x^M}{C_n^N}$$

where

M = Population nonconformances

N = Population size

n = Sample size

x = Number of occurrences in a sample

V.E.2

60. a; An independent event is one in which its occurrence has no effect on the probability of the other event or events. The multiplicative law of probability applies in this case.

    Theorem 6. If A and B are independent events (one where its occurrence has no influence on the probability of the other event or events), then the probability of both A and B occurring is the product of their respective probabilities: P(A and B) = P(A) × P(B). [V.E.1]

61. a; An independent event is one in which its occurrence has no effect on the probability of the other event or events.

    Theorem 6. If A and B are independent events (one where its occurrence has no influence on the probability of the other event or events), then the probability of both A and B occurring is the product of their respective probabilities: P(A and B) = P(A) × P(B). [V.E.1]

62. d; A combination is a counting technique that requires the unordered arrangement of a set of objects.

$$C(n,k) = \frac{n!}{(n-k)!k!}$$

    where C is the number of ways to combine k items from a set of n. [V.E.1]

63. c; The main difference between a permutation and a combination is that order is important in a permutation, but not in a combination. [V.E.1]

64. c; Venn diagrams are used to graphically display collections of sets and represent their relationships.

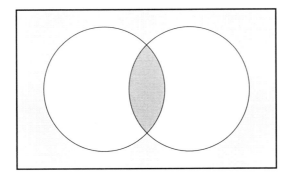

V.E.1

65. d; The normal distribution is used for continuous data.

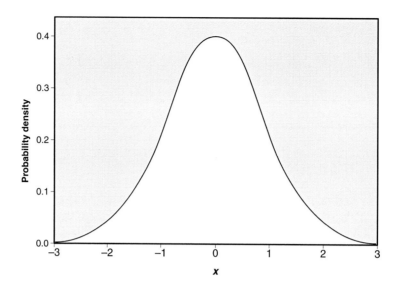

[V.E.2]

66. c; If something has a "fifty-fifty chance" of occurring, the probability that it will occur is 0.5 or 50%.

Theorem 1. Probability is expressed as a number between 1 and 0, where a value of 1 is a certainty that an event will occur and a value of 0 is a certainty that an event will not occur. [V.E.1]

67. b; If a tray holds 30 parts, of which there are six defective parts, and sample one part from the tray, the probability that it will be a defective part is calculated by

$$P_{Tray} = \frac{30}{30} = 1.0 \text{ or } 100\%$$

$$P_{Good} = \frac{24}{30} = 0.8 \text{ or } 80\%$$

$$P_{Bad} = \frac{6}{30} = 0.2 \text{ or } 20\%$$

If one part is drawn at random is defective is 20%. [V.E.1]

68. d; A newly formed ASQ Section consists of 12 members. 1320 slates of officers could be formed for the offices of chair, vice chair, and secretary.

This is a simple calculation on a standard scientific calculator: 12 permutation 3 = 1320. [V.E.1]

69. c; A project team consists of 12 members. 220 subcommittees of three can be formed.

     This is a simple calculation on a standard scientific calculator: 12 combination 3 = 220. [V.E.1]

70. c; A coil of steel has an overage of five nonconformances. What is the probability of three nonconformances in a randomly selected coil?

     This is an application of the Poisson distribution.

     $$P(x) = \frac{e^{-\mu}\mu^{x}}{x!}$$

     where

     $e = 2.71828\ldots$, the base of natural logarithms

     μ = The expected number of occurrences

     x = Number of occurrences during this trial

     $$P(x) = \frac{e^{-\mu}\mu^{x}}{x!} = \frac{e^{-5}5^{3}}{3!} = 0.14 \text{ or } 14\%$$

     [V.E.2]

71. d; If there are five different parts to be stocked, but only three bins available, what is the number of permutations of the five parts in the three bins? There are 60 permutations of the five parts in the three bins.

     This is a simple calculation on a standard scientific calculator: 5 permutation 3 = 60. [V.E.1]

72. a; A sample of three numbers is selected from the numbers 1 to 45. How many different combinations are possible? There are 14,190 combinations possible.

     This is a simple calculation on a standard scientific calculator: 45 combination 3 = 14,190. [V.E.1]

73. b; The probability of selecting two nonconforming units in a sample of four circuit boards from a steady stream of circuit boards that is known to be 12% nonconforming is 0.067.

     This is an application of the binomial distribution.

     $$P(x) = C_{X}^{n}p^{x}(1-p)^{n-x}$$

where

p = Probability of occurrence

$1 - p$ = Probability of nonoccurrence

n = Sample size

x = Number of occurrences in n trials

$$P(x) = C_X^n p^x (1-p)^{n-x} = P(x) = C_2^4 0.12^2 (1-0.12)^{4-2} = 0.067 \text{ or } 6.7\%$$

[V.E.2]

74. c; An inspector randomly selects three parts from a lot of 20 that is known to be 10% nonconforming. What is the probability that the selected samples will contain no nonconforming units?

This is an application of the hypergeometric distribution.

$$P(x) = \frac{C_{n-x}^{N-M} C_x^M}{C_n^N}$$

where

M = Population nonconformances

N = Population size

n = Sample size

x = Number of occurrences in a sample

$$P(x) = \frac{C_{n-x}^{N-M} C_x^M}{C_n^N} = \frac{C_{3-0}^{20-2} C_0^2}{C_3^{20}} = 0.176 \text{ or } 17.6\%$$

[V.E.2]

75. a; The most desirable relationship between the specification and the process spread is when $6\sigma <$ USL – LSL, as demonstrated in the figure below.

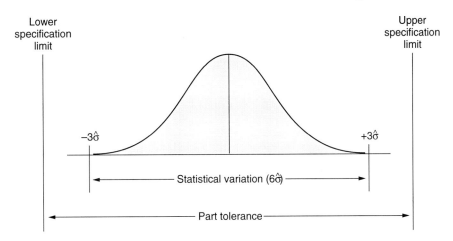

Relationship between statistical control limits and product specifications.

Source: Adapted from Durivage (2014). Used with permission.

[V.F.1]

76. b; By definition, the larger the value, the more capable the process.

$$C_p = \frac{USL - LSL}{6s} > 1$$

[V.F.1]

77. a; The least desirable relationship between the specification and the process spread is when $6\sigma <$ USL – LSL, as demonstrated in the figure below.

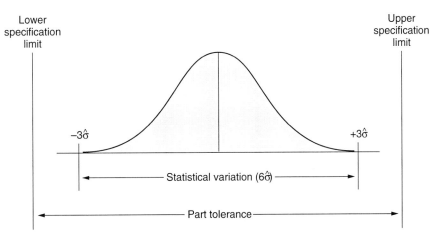

Relationship between statistical control limits and product specifications.

Source: Adapted from Durivage (2014). Used with permission.

[V.F.1]

78. d; The process spread is simply the amount of variation present in the process. [V.F.1]

79. a; The numerator of the capability index equation is the tolerance.

$$C_p = \frac{USL - LSL}{6s} > 1$$

[V.F.1]

80. a; The capability ratio is calculated by the following formula:

$$C_r = \frac{6s}{USL - LSL}$$

Given USL 950, LSL 850, s 15.85,

$$C_r = \frac{6 \times 15.85}{950 - 850} = 0.951$$

A C_r ratio of less than 1 is considered capable.

[V.F.1]

81. b; The capability index is calculated by the following formula:

$$C_p = \frac{USL - LSL}{6s}$$

Given USL 950, LSL 850, s 15.85,

$$C_p = \frac{950 - 850}{6 \times 15.85} = 1.052$$

A C_p ratio greater than 1 is considered capable.

[V.F.1]

82. c; The process capability ratio is calculated by the following formula:

$$C_{pk} = \text{Minimum of } \frac{\bar{X} - LSL}{3s}, \frac{USL - \bar{X}}{3s}$$

Given $\bar{\bar{X}}$ 904.573, USL 950, LSL 850, s 15.85,

$$\frac{904.573 - 850}{3 \times 15.85} = 1.148, \quad \frac{950 - 904.573}{3 \times 15.85} = 0.955$$

The smaller value is selected (0.955). A C_{pk} ratio of less than 1 is considered not capable. One possible remedy would be to center the process. [V.F.1]

83. c; The process capability on an attributes control chart is simply the centerline of the control chart (process average). [V.F.4]

84. d; If the C_{pk} = 0.85 and C_p = 1.1, the process is narrow enough to be capable, but is not centered.

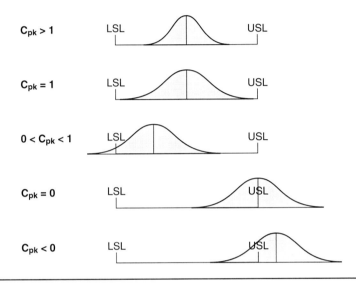

Source: Adapted from Durivage (2014).

[V.F.1]

85. b; To calculate the process capability for a *p*-chart, the centerline must be first be calculated using the following formula:

$$\bar{p} = \frac{\Sigma np}{\Sigma n} \text{ (Centerline)}$$

where

   n = Subgroup size

   k = The number of subgroups

Given the sum *np* 55, sum of *n* 2800,

$$\bar{p} = \frac{55}{2800} = 0.020$$

For attributes control charts, the process capability is simply the centerline of the control chart, in this case, 0.020. [V.F.4]

86. c; To calculate the process capability for an *np*-chart, the centerline must be first be calculated using the following formula:

$$\overline{np} = \frac{\Sigma np}{k} \text{ (Centerline)}$$

where

n = Subgroup size

np = (Subgroup count)

k = The number of subgroups

Given the sum of *np* 55, *k* 14,

$$\overline{np} = \frac{55}{14} = 3.929$$

For attributes control charts, the process capability is simply the centerline of the control chart, in this case 3.929. [V.F.4]

87. b; To calculate the process capability for a *c*-chart, the centerline must be first be calculated using the following formula:

$$\overline{c} = \frac{\Sigma c}{k} \text{ (Centerline)}$$

where

c = (Subgroup count)

k = The number of subgroups

Given the sum of *c* 37 and *k* 14,

$$\overline{c} = \frac{37}{14} = 2.642$$

For attributes control charts, the process capability is simply the centerline of the control chart, in this case 2.642. [V.F.4]

88. b; To calculate the process capability for a u-chart, the centerline must first be calculated using the following formula:

$$\bar{u} = \frac{\Sigma c}{\Sigma n} \text{ (Centerline)}$$

where

    n = Subgroup size

    k = The number of subgroups

Given the sum of c 244 and sum of n 112,

$$\bar{u} = \frac{244}{112} = 2.179$$

For attributes control charts, the process capability is simply the centerline of the control chart, in this case, 2.179. [V.F.4]

Part VI

Analyze

(44 questions)

A. MEASURING AND MODELING RELATIONSHIPS BETWEEN VARIABLES

1. *Correlation coefficient.* Calculate and interpret the correlation coefficient and its confidence interval, and describe the difference between correlation and causation. (Evaluate)

2. *Linear regression.* Calculate and interpret regression analysis, and apply and interpret hypothesis tests for regression statistics. Use the regression model for estimation and prediction, analyze the uncertainty in the estimate, and perform a residuals analysis to validate the model. (Evaluate)

3. *Multivariate tools.* Use and interpret multivariate tools (e.g., factor analysis, discriminant analysis, multiple analysis of variance (MANOVA)) to investigate sources of variation. (Evaluate)

B. HYPOTHESIS TESTING

1. *Terminology.* Define and interpret the significance level, power, type I, and type II errors of statistical tests. (Evaluate)

2. *Statistical vs. practical significance.* Define, compare, and interpret statistical and practical significance. (Evaluate)

3. *Sample size.* Calculate sample size for common hypothesis tests: equality of means and equality of proportions. (Apply)

4. *Point and interval estimates.* Define and distinguish between confidence and prediction intervals. Define and interpret the efficiency and bias of estimators. Calculate tolerance and confidence intervals. (Evaluate)

5. *Tests for means, variances, and proportions.* Use and interpret the results of hypothesis tests for means, variances, and proportions. (Evaluate)

6. *Analysis of variance (ANOVA).* Select, calculate, and interpret the results of ANOVAs. (Evaluate)

7. *Goodness-of-fit (chi square) tests.* Define, select, and interpret the results of these tests. (Evaluate)

8. *Contingency tables.* Select, develop, and use contingency tables to determine statistical significance. (Evaluate)

9. *Non-parametric tests.* Understand the importance of the Kruskal-Wallis and Mann-Whitney tests and when they should be used. (Understand)

C. FAILURE MODE AND EFFECTS ANALYSIS (FMEA)

Describe the purpose and elements of FMEA, including risk priority number (RPN), and evaluate FMEA results for processes, products, and services. Distinguish between design FMEA (DFMEA) and process FMEA (PFMEA), and interpret their results. (Evaluate)

D. ADDITIONAL ANALYSIS METHODS

1. *Gap analysis.* Analyze scenarios to identify performance gaps, and compare current and future states using predefined metrics. (Analyze)

2. *Root cause analysis.* Define and describe the purpose of root cause analysis, recognize the issues involved in identifying a root cause, and use various tools (e.g., 5 whys, Pareto charts, fault tree analysis, cause and effect diagrams) to resolve chronic problems. (Analyze)

3. *Waste analysis.* Identify and interpret the seven classic wastes (overproduction, inventory, defects, over-processing, waiting, motion, transportation) and resource under-utilization. (Analyze)

QUESTIONS

Use the figure below to answer questions 1–4.

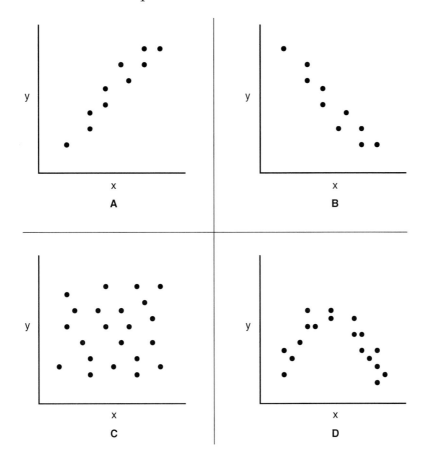

1. Which figure demonstrates perfect negative correlation?

   a. Figure A

   b. Figure B

   c. Figure C

   d. Figure D

2. Which figure demonstrates nonlinear correlation?

   a. Figure A

   b. Figure B

   c. Figure C

   d. Figure D

3. Which figure demonstrates no correlation?

    a. Figure A

    b. Figure B

    c. Figure C

    d. Figure D

4. Which figure demonstrates positive correlation?

    a. Figure A

    b. Figure B

    c. Figure C

    d. Figure D

Use the table below to answer questions 5–11.

Time	Strength				
X	Y	XY	X^2	Y^2	
1.0	41	41	1.0	1681	
1.5	41	61.5	2.3	1681	
2.0	41	82	4.0	1681	
2.5	43	107.5	6.3	1849	
3.0	43	129	9.0	1849	
3.5	44	154	12.3	1936	
4.0	50	200	16.0	2500	
17.5	**303.0**	**775.0**	**50.8**	**13177.0**	**Sum**

5. What is the correlation coefficient?

    a. 17.50

    b. 0.710

    c. 1.000

    d. 0.843

6. What is the coefficient of determination?

    a. 17.50

    b. 0.710

    c. 1.000

    d. 0.843

7. What is the number of paired samples?

   a. Two

   b. Seven

   c. Eight

   d. 14

8. What is the slope of the regression line?

   a. 1.00

   b. 2.48

   c. 7.00

   d. −7.00

9. What is the y intercept point?

   a. 37.086

   b. 27.065

   c. 28.614

   d. 1.00

10. What is the equation of the line?

   a. $Y = 37.086X + 2.48$

   b. $Y = 2.48X + 1.00$

   c. $Y = -X + 37.086$

   d. $Y = 2.48X + 37.086$

11. What is the expected output if a time of 7.0 seconds is used?

   a. 50

   b. 54

   c. 60

   d. 63

12. What type of error is rejecting the null when the null is true?

   a. Type I

   b. Type II

Part VI
Questions

c. Type III

d. Type IV

13. What type of error is failing to reject the null when the null is false?

    a. Type I

    b. Type II

    c. Type III

    d. Type IV

14. A Six Sigma professional wants to determine with 95% confidence whether the mean fill weight differs by 1 g after making an adjustment to the process. The process historical $\sigma = 3.5$ g. What is the minimum required sample size?

    a. 48

    b. 53

    c. 60

    d. 90

15. A process has an average of 1.500 for the last 50 parts produced, and a historical standard deviation of 0.002. Find the 95% prediction interval for the next part produced.

    a. 1.406 and 1.504

    b. 1.396 and 1.521

    c. 1.496 and 1.504

    d. 1.596 and 1.704

16. A process has an average of 1.500 and a sample standard deviation of 0.002. If 500 parts are produced, what is the tolerance interval that we can be 95% confident will contain 99% of the products produced?

    a. 1.406 and 1.504

    b. 1.396 and 1.521

    c. 1.495 and 1.505

    d. 1.596 and 1.704

17. If the mean of a sample drawn from a population is 2.15, and the population standard deviation is known to be 0.8, calculate the 95% confidence interval for the average if the sample size is 75.

   a. 1.969 to 2.331

   b. 1.960 to 2.333

   c. 1.979 to 2.341

   d. 1.996 to 2.427

18. To compare the means of three or more groups simultaneously, which of the following tests is the most appropriate?

   a. Student's t-test

   b. Fischer's exact test

   c. Chi-squared test

   d. ANOVA

Use the following table to answer questions 19 and 20.

One-Way ANOVA Summary Table					
Source of variation	SS	df	MS	F calculated	F critical
Between groups	46.8		23.4	10.97	3.89
Within groups (error)	25.6		2.1		
Total	72.4				

19. Using the One-Way ANOVA Summary Table, which of the following correctly completes the degrees of freedom?

   a. 1, 11, 12

   b. 1, 12, 13

   c. 2, 11, 13

   d. 2, 12, 14

20. Using the One-Way ANOVA Summary Table, which of the following statements is correct?

   a. There is insufficient evidence to reject the null hypothesis.

   b. There is sufficient evidence to reject the null hypothesis.

   c. There is sufficient evidence to accept the null hypothesis.

   d. There is insufficient evidence to accept the null hypothesis.

21. With n observations from a random sample, each of which could be classified into exactly one of K categories, how many degrees of freedom does a goodness-of-fit test with specified probabilities have?

    a. K

    b. $K + 1$

    c. $K - 1$

    d. $K - 2$

22. When testing for the independence in a contingency table with four rows and three columns, calculate the degrees of freedom for the test statistic.

    a. 6

    b. 7

    c. 11

    d. 12

23. A process improvement team has completed a PFMEA. Which of the following tools would be best suited to help the team focus their efforts based on the PFMEA?

    a. SWOT analysis

    b. Pareto analysis

    c. Force-field analysis

    d. Statistical analysis

24. A value indicating the relative risk of a potential failure is referred to as:

    a. failure.

    b. modality.

    c. RPN.

    d. severity.

25. An FMEA has a severity of 7, a probability of occurrence of 5, and a probability of detection of 3. What is the RPN?

    a. 12

    b. 15

c. 35

d. 105

26. A systematic approach that proactively identifies, analyzes, prioritizes, and documents potential failure modes and their respective potential causes of failures is:

    a. DFSS.

    b. FMEA.

    c. SIPOC.

    d. PDCA.

27. The likelihood that current controls will prevent a failure from reaching the customer is called:

    a. detection.

    b. occurrence.

    c. severity.

    d. FMEA.

28. A tool used in the design process to minimize or prevent failures, and improve safety and quality is:

    a. SWOT.

    b. PDCA.

    c. DFSS.

    d. FMEA.

29. A Six Sigma team has been charged with the task of redesigning a product and reducing the overall risk to the end user. Which of the following tools would be the most appropriate for the team to use?

    a. PDCA

    b. DOE

    c. FMEA

    d. SWOT

Use the following FMEA to answer questions 30–33.

Row	Current process				Action results			
	Severity	Occurrence	Detection	RPN	Severity	Occurrence	Detection	RPN
1	3	5	10	150	3	5	3	45
2	5	10	3	150	3	5	3	45
3	10	3	5	150	10	3	1	30

30. On which row of the FMEA should a process improvement team focus their efforts for the current state of the process?

    a. 1

    b. 2

    c. 3

    d. The RPNs are the same, no special effort is necessary.

31. Rank the order of risk for the current state of the process:

    a. 3, 2, 1

    b. 2, 3, 1

    c. 1, 2, 3

    d. The RPNs are the same, therefore the risk is the same.

32. What is the overall percentage of RPN reduction in row 1?

    a. 30%

    b. 45%

    c. 55%

    d. 70%

33. What is the overall percentage of RPN reduction in row 3?

    a. 20%

    b. 30%

    c. 80%

    d. 85%

34. The causal factor or factors that, if removed, will prevent the recurrence of the same situation describe:

    a. process control.

    b. root cause.

    c. root cause analysis.

    d. FMEA.

35. A tool used to provide visual identification of many potential causes of a problem is the:

    a. decision tree.

    b. process flowchart.

    c. cause-and-effect diagram.

    d. check sheet.

Use the following diagram to answer questions 36–39.

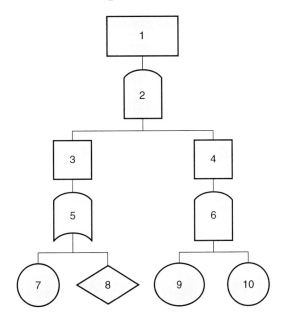

36. Which of the FTA symbols indicates an AND gate?

    a. 2

    b. 5

    c. 6

    d. 2 and 6

37. Which of the FTA symbols indicates an OR gate?

    a. 2

    b. 5

    c. 6

    d. 5 and 6

38. Which of the FTA symbols indicates an undeveloped event?

    a. 7

    b. 8

    c. 9

    d. 7 and 10

39. Which of the FTA symbols indicates the primary event?

    a. 1

    b. 3

    c. 4

    d. 3 and 4

40. The phrase "vital few and useful many" is applicable to the:

    a. cause-and-effect diagram.

    b. check sheet.

    c. Pareto diagram.

    d. process flow diagram.

41. When constructing a Pareto diagram, where is the "other" category placed?

    a. First column.

    b. Last column.

    c. Depends on the number of other items.

    d. The "other" column should not be used.

Use the following paragraph to answer questions 42–44.

ABC Manufacturing, a machine shop that uses total productive maintenance methodologies, received a purchase order from their customer for 50 parts. Because of ABC's experience with manufacturing and the long lead time to produce these parts, ABC creates a production order for 55 parts to ensure that they will complete at least 50 parts.

42. Producing 55 parts when the order was for 50 is an example of what type of waste?

    a. Processing

    b. Inventory

    c. Defects

    d. Overproduction

43. ABC is actively eliminating what type of waste?

    a. Inventory

    b. Processing

    c. Waiting

    d. Transportation

44. It can be assumed that the most likely reason ABC is producing 55 parts instead of 50 parts is due to what type of waste?

    a. Overproduction

    b. Defects

    c. Transportation

    d. Inventory

ANSWERS

1. b; This figure demonstrates nearly perfect negative correlation. The points fall on a straight line decreasing from left to right. [VI.A.1]

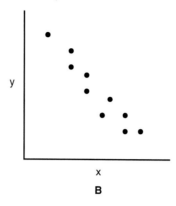

2. d; This figure demonstrates nonlinear correlation (quadratic correlation). There are times when there can be linear, quadratic, cubic, or no correlation present. [VI.A.1]

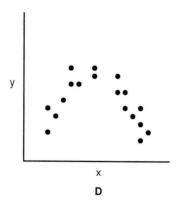

3. c; This figure has no discernable relationship. Therefore, there is no correlation present between the two variables. [VI.A.1]

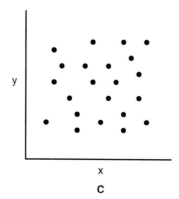

4. a; This figure demonstrates positive correlation. The points fall on a straight line increasing from left to right. However, the correlation is not perfect due to the width (dispersion) of the points. [VI.A.1]

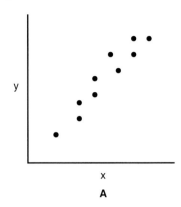

A

5. d; The correlation coefficient is calculated using the following formula:

$$r = \frac{n \times \Sigma XY - \Sigma X \times \Sigma Y}{\sqrt{n \times \Sigma X^2 - (\Sigma x)^2} \times \sqrt{n \times \Sigma Y^2 - (\Sigma Y)^2}}$$

where

r = Correlation coefficient

X = The independent variable

Y = The dependent variable

n = The number of sample pairs

Time	Strength				
X	Y	XY	X²	Y²	
1.0	41	41	1.0	1681	
1.5	41	61.5	2.3	1681	
2.0	41	82	4.0	1681	
2.5	43	107.5	6.3	1849	
3.0	43	129	9.0	1849	
3.5	44	154	12.3	1936	
4.0	50	200	16.0	2500	
17.5	**303.0**	**775.0**	**50.8**	**13177.0**	**Sum**

$$r = \frac{7 \times 775 - 17.5 \times 303}{\sqrt{7 \times 50.8 - (17.5)^2} \times \sqrt{7 \times 13177 - (303)^2}} = 0.843$$

[VI.A.1]

6. b; The coefficient of determination is the correlation coefficient squared:

$$r^2 = 0.710$$

[VI.A.1]

7. b; The table below contains seven paired samples.

Time	Strength				
X	Y	XY	X²	Y²	
1.0	41	41	1.0	1681	
1.5	41	61.5	2.3	1681	
2.0	41	82	4.0	1681	
2.5	43	107.5	6.3	1849	
3.0	43	129	9.0	1849	
3.5	44	154	12.3	1936	
4.0	50	200	16.0	2500	
17.5	303.0	775.0	50.8	13177.0	Sum

[VI.A.2]

8. b; Regression analyses assess the association between two variables and define their relationship. The general equation for a line is given by

$$Y = aX + b$$

where

$$a = \frac{n \times \Sigma XY - \Sigma X \times \Sigma Y}{n \times \Sigma X^2 - (\Sigma X)^2}$$

and

$$b = \frac{\Sigma Y - a \times \Sigma X}{n}$$

where

X = The independent variable

Y = The dependent variable

n = The number of sample pairs

a = The slope of the regression line

b = The intercept point on the Y-axis

Time	Strength				
X	Y	XY	X²	Y²	
1.0	41	41	1.0	1681	
1.5	41	61.5	2.3	1681	
2.0	41	82	4.0	1681	
2.5	43	107.5	6.3	1849	
3.0	43	129	9.0	1849	
3.5	44	154	12.3	1936	
4.0	50	200	16.0	2500	
17.5	**303.0**	**775.0**	**50.8**	**13177.0**	**Sum**

Using the data from the table above, the slope of the regression line is calculated as

$$a = \frac{n \times \Sigma XY - \Sigma X \times \Sigma Y}{n \times \Sigma X^2 - (\Sigma X)^2} = \frac{7 \times 775 - 17.5 \times 303}{7 \times 50.8 - 17.5^2} = 2.48$$

[VI.A.2]

9. a; Regression analyses assess the association between two variables and define their relationship. The general equation for a line is given by

$$Y = aX + b$$

where

$$a = \frac{n \times \Sigma XY - \Sigma X \times \Sigma Y}{n \times \Sigma X^2 - (\Sigma X)^2}$$

and

$$b = \frac{\Sigma Y - a \times \Sigma X}{n}$$

where

X = The independent variable

Y = The dependent variable

n = The number of sample pairs

a = The slope of the regression line

b = The intercept point on the Y-axis

Time	Strength				
X	Y	XY	X²	Y²	
1.0	41	41	1.0	1681	
1.5	41	61.5	2.3	1681	
2.0	41	82	4.0	1681	
2.5	43	107.5	6.3	1849	
3.0	43	129	9.0	1849	
3.5	44	154	12.3	1936	
4.0	50	200	16.0	2500	
17.5	**303.0**	**775.0**	**50.8**	**13177.0**	**Sum**

Using the data from the table above, the y intercept point is calculated as

$$b = \frac{\Sigma Y - a \times \Sigma X}{n} = \frac{303 - 2.48 \times 17.5}{7} = 37.086$$

[VI.A.2]

10. d; Putting the calculated values into the standard form will yield the following regression line:

$$Y = 2.48X + 37.086$$

[VI.A.2]

11. b; The expected output at a time of 7.0 seconds is calculated by using the following standard form of the regression line:

$$Y = 2.48X + 37.086 = 2.48(7) + 37.086 = 54$$

The expected strength is 54. [VI.A.2]

12. b; Type I error occurs when the null hypothesis is rejected when it is true. We refer to the P(Type I error) = P(Rejecting H_0 when H_0 is true) = α. A type I error is also known as an α *error* and an *error of the first kind*. The P(Type I error) is also known as α-*value, producer's risk, level of significance,* and *significance level.*

		Nature (true condition)	
		H_0 is true	H_0 is false
Conclusion	H_0 is rejected	Type I error P(Type I)	**Correct decision**
	H_0 is not rejected	**Correct decision**	Type II error P(Type II)

[V1.B.1]

13. a; Type II error occurs when the alternative hypothesis is not rejected when it is false. We refer to the P(Type II error) = P(Not rejecting H_0 when H_0 is false) = β. A type II error is also known as a β *error* and an *error of the second kind.*

		Nature (true condition)	
		H_0 is true	H_0 is false
Conclusion	H_0 is rejected	Type I error P(Type I) = a	**Correct decision**
	H_0 is not rejected	**Correct decision**	Type II error P(Type II)

[VI.B.1]

14. a; To calculate the minimum sample size required with 95% confidence if the mean fill weight differs by 1 g after making an adjustment to the process (historical σ = 3.5g), use the following formula:

$$n = \left(\frac{z_{\alpha/2}\sigma}{E} \right)^2$$

where

σ = Standard deviation

E = Difference to detect

$z_{\alpha/2}$ = The normal distribution value for a given confidence level

$n = (1.96 \times 3.51)^2 = 47.33$, rounded up 48

48 samples are needed to detect a difference of 1 g for a process with a historical standard deviation of 3.5.

See Appendix D, Selected Single-Sided Normal Distribution Probability Points Factors from Durivage (2014). [VI.B.3]

15. c; A process has an average of 1.500 for the last 50 parts produced, and a historical standard deviation of 0.002. The 95% prediction interval is calculated by

$$\bar{X} \pm Z_{\alpha/2} \times \sigma \times \sqrt{1 + \frac{1}{n}}$$

where

σ = Standard deviation

$\bar{X}$ = The sample mean

n = Sample size

$Z_{\alpha/2}$ = The normal distribution value for a given confidence level.

$$\bar{X} \pm Z_{\alpha/2} \times \sigma \times \sqrt{1 + \frac{1}{n}}$$

$$1.500 \pm 1.960 \times 0.002 \times \sqrt{1 + \frac{1}{50}} = 0.004$$

$$1.500 \pm 0.004 = 1.496 \text{ to } 1.504$$

We can be 95% confident the next part will fall between 1.496 and 1.504.

See Appendix D, Selected Single-Sided Normal Distribution Probability Points Factors from Durivage (2014). [VI.B.4]

16. c; A process has an average of 1.500 and a sample standard deviation of 0.002. If 500 parts are produced, the tolerance interval that we can be 95% confident will contain 99% of the products produced is calculated by

$$\bar{X} \pm K_2 s \text{ Two-sided bilateral limits}$$

where

K_2 = Two-sided factor

s = Sample standard deviation

$\bar{X}$ = The sample mean

$$\bar{X} \pm K_2 s$$

$$1.500 \pm 2.721 \times 0.002 = 0.005$$

$$1.500 \pm 0.005 = 1.495 \text{ to } 1.505$$

We can be 95% confident that 99% of the parts are between 1.495 and 1.505.

See Appendix H, Tolerance Interval Factors from Durivage (2014). [VI.B.4]

17. a; To calculate the 95% confidence interval for the average if the sample size is 75, the mean of a sample drawn from a population is 2.15, and the population standard deviation is known to be 0.8, use

$$\bar{X} \pm Z_{\alpha/2} \frac{\sigma}{\sqrt{n}}$$

where

X = The point estimate of the average

σ = The population standard deviation

n = The sample size

$Z_{\alpha/2}$ = The normal distribution value for a given confidence level

See Appendix D, Selected Double-Sided Normal Distribution Probability Points from Durivage (2014).

$$\bar{X} \pm Z_{\alpha/2} \frac{\sigma}{\sqrt{n}} = 2.15 \pm 1.960 \times \frac{0.8}{\sqrt{75}} = 2.15 \pm 0.181 = 1.969 \text{ to } 2.331$$

The 95% confidence interval is 1.969 to 2.331. [VI.B.4]

18. d; To compare the means of three or more groups simultaneously, an ANOVA is the most appropriate test. In its simplest form, ANOVA provides a statistical test of whether or not the means of three or more groups are equal, and therefore generalizes the *t*-test to more than two groups. Doing multiple two-sample *t*-tests would result in an increased chance of committing a type I error. For this reason, ANOVAs are useful in comparing three or more means for statistical significance. [VI.B.6]

19. d; To calculate the degrees of freedom from the information provided, use

$$df = SS/MS$$

One-Way ANOVA Summary Table					
Source of variation	SS	df	MS	*F* calculated	*F* critical
Between groups	46.8		23.4	10.97	3.89
Within groups (error)	25.6		2.1		
Total	72.4				

Between groups:

$$df = \frac{46.8}{23.4} = 2$$

Within groups (error):

$$df = \frac{25.6}{2.1} = 12$$

Total *df* = 2 + 12 = 14.

Between groups 2, within groups (error) 12, total 14. [VI.B.6]

20. b; Based on the One-Way ANOVA Summary Table, since *F* calculated is greater than *F* critical, there is sufficient evidence to reject the null hypothesis.

One-Way ANOVA Summary Table					
Source of variation	SS	df	MS	*F* calculated	*F* critical
Between groups	46.8		23.4	10.97	3.89
Within groups (error)	25.6		2.1		
Total	72.4				

[VI.B.6]

21. c; The number of degrees of freedom with *n* observations from a random sample, each of which could be classified into exactly one of *K* categories for a goodness-of-fit test with specified probabilities, is calculated by $(k - 1)$. [VI.B.7]

22. a; A contingency table contains four rows and three columns. The degrees of freedom for the test statistic is calculated by

$$df = (r - 1)(c - 1) = (4 - 1)(3 - 1) = 6$$

[VI.B.8]

23. b; A Pareto chart can be used to help a process improvement team focus their efforts based on the PFMEA. [VI.C]

24. c; The RPN 24 is a value indicating the relative risk of the potential failure. The RPN is the product of the severity, probability of occurrence, and probability of detection. [VI.C]

25. d; To calculate the RPN for an FMEA with a severity of 7, a probability of occurrence of 5, and a probability of detection of 3, the following formula is used:

$$RPN = S \times O \times D = 7 \times 5 \times 3 = 105$$

where

S = Severity

O = Probability of occurrence

D = Probability of detection

[VI.C]

26. b; FMEA is a systematic approach that proactively identifies, analyzes, prioritizes, and documents potential failure modes and their respective potential causes of failures. [VI.C]

27. a; Detection is the likelihood that current controls will prevent a failure from reaching the customer. [VI.C]

28. d; FMEA is used in the design process to minimize or prevent failures, and improve safety and quality. [VI.C]

29. c; The most appropriate tool for a Six Sigma team charged with the task of redesigning a product and reducing the overall risk to the end user would be FMEA. [VI.C]

30. c; The process improvement team should first focus their efforts on the current state of the process for row 3, as row 3 has the highest severity (10).

	Current process				Action results			
Row	Severity	Occurrence	Detection	RPN	Severity	Occurrence	Detection	RPN
1	3	5	10	150	3	5	3	45
2	5	10	3	150	3	5	3	45
3	10	3	5	150	10	3	1	30

[VI.C]

31. a; The order of risk for the current state of the process is row 3, row 2, and row 1. All three rows have the same RPN. Based on the information provided, the risk priority will be determined by the severity.

	Current process				Action results			
Row	Severity	Occurrence	Detection	RPN	Severity	Occurrence	Detection	RPN
1	3	5	10	150	3	5	3	45
2	5	10	3	150	3	5	3	45
3	10	3	5	150	10	3	1	30

[VI.C]

32. d; The percentage of RPN reduction in row 1 is calculated by the formula

$$\% \text{ RPN Reduction} = \frac{\text{RPN}_i - \text{RPN}_r}{\text{RPN}_i} = (150 - 45)/150 = 0.70 \text{ or } 70\%$$

where

RPN$_i$ = Initial RPN

RPN$_r$ = Revised RPN

	Current process				Action results			
Row	Severity	Occurrence	Detection	RPN	Severity	Occurrence	Detection	RPN
1	3	5	10	150	3	5	3	45
2	5	10	3	150	3	5	3	45
3	10	3	5	150	10	3	1	30

[VI.C]

33. c; The percentage of RPN reduction in row 1 is calculated by the formula

$$\% \ \text{RPN Reduction} = \frac{\text{RPN}_i - \text{RPN}_r}{\text{RPN}_i} = (150-30)/150 = 0.80 \text{ or } 80\%$$

where

RPN_i = Initial RPN

RPN_r = Revised RPN

$$\% \ \text{RPN Reduction} = \frac{\text{RPN}_i - \text{RPN}_r}{\text{RPN}_i}$$

	Current process				Action results			
Row	Severity	Occurrence	Detection	RPN	Severity	Occurrence	Detection	RPN
1	3	5	10	150	3	5	3	45
2	5	10	3	150	3	5	3	45
3	10	3	5	150	10	3	1	30

[VI.C]

34. b; Solving a process problem means identifying the root cause and eliminating it.

   The ultimate test of whether the root cause has been eliminated is the ability to toggle the problem on and off by removing and reintroducing the root cause. [VI.D.2]

35. c; A cause-and-effect diagram (also called an *Ishikawa diagram* or *fishbone diagram*) traditionally divides causes into several generic categories. In use, a large empty diagram is often drawn on a whiteboard or flip chart to visually display potential causes of a problem. [VI.D.2]

36. d; Numbers 2 and 6 represent AND gates.

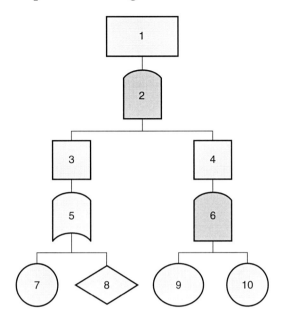

[VI.D.2]

37. b; Number 5 represents an OR gate.

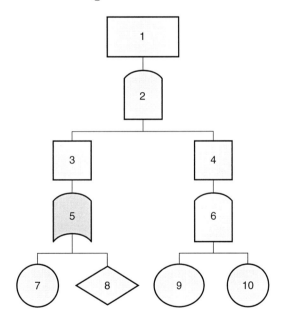

[VI.D.2]

38. b; Number 8 represents an undeveloped event.

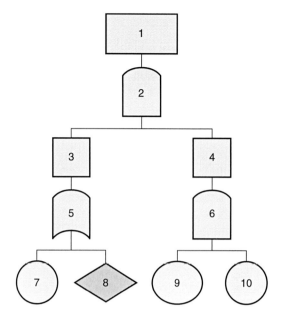

[VI.D.2]

39. a; Number 1 represents a primary event.

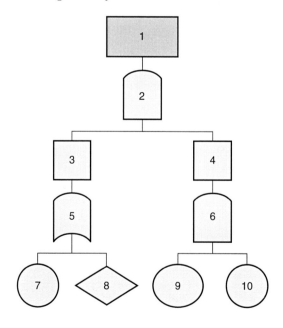

[VI.D.2]

40. c; The purpose of the Pareto chart is to separate the "vital few" causes from the "trivial many." This is often reflected in what is called the 80/20 rule, and helps focus attention on the more pressing issues. [VI.D.2]

41. b; When constructing a Pareto chart, the "other" category is placed in the last column. Because there are many types of minor defects that are few in quantity, they are collected in this category. There is no real need to identify them by specific type since they make up the trivial many and will not be investigated. [VI.D.2]

42. d; ABC producing 55 parts when the order is for 50 is an example of overproduction. Overproduction is considered to be a form of waste. [VI.D.3]

43. c; ABC is actively eliminating waiting time. Waiting time is considered to be a form of waste. [VI.D.3]

44. b; ABC is producing 55 parts instead of 50 parts due to defects. The overproduction of parts is considered to be a form of waste. [VI.D.3]

Part VI
Answers

Part VII

Improve

(54 questions)

A. DESIGN OF EXPERIMENTS (DOE)

1. *Terminology.* Define basic DOE terms, e.g., independent and dependent variables, factors and levels, response, treatment, error, nested. (Understand)

2. *Design principles.* Define and apply DOE principles, e.g., power, sample size, balance, repetition, replication, order, efficiency, randomization, blocking, interaction, confounding, resolution. (Apply)

3. *Planning experiments.* Plan and evaluate DOEs by determining the objective, selecting appropriate factors, responses, and measurement methods, and choosing the appropriate design. (Evaluate)

4. *One-factor experiments.* Design and conduct completely randomized, randomized block, and Latin square designs, and evaluate their results. (Evaluate)

5. *Two-level fractional factorial experiments.* Design, analyze, and interpret these types of experiments, and describe how confounding can affect their use. (Evaluate)

6. *Full factorial experiments.* Design, conduct, and analyze these types of experiments. (Evaluate)

B. LEAN METHODS

1. *Waste elimination.* Select and apply tools and techniques for eliminating or preventing waste, e.g., pull systems, kanban, 5S, standard work, poka-yoke. (Analyze)

2. *Cycle-time reduction.* Use various tools and techniques for reducing cycle time, e.g., continuous flow, single-minute exchange of die (SMED), heijunka (production leveling). (Analyze)

3. *Kaizen.* Define and distinguish between kaizen and kaizen blitz and describe when to use each method. (Apply)

4. *Other improvement tools and techniques.* Identify and describe how other process improvement methodologies are used, e.g., theory of constraints (TOC), overall equipment effectiveness (OEE). (Understand)

C. IMPLEMENTATION

Develop plans for implementing proposed improvements, including conducting pilot tests or simulations, and evaluate results to select the optimum solution. (Evaluate)

QUESTIONS

1. A study was conducted with three replicates of two treatments. The variation in the readings of the three replicates is known as:

    a. error.

    b. interaction.

    c. noise.

    d. capability.

2. What experimental design technique would be used when an experiment may have to be conducted over several shifts?

    a. Blocking

    b. Confounding

    c. Replication

    d. Randomization

3. An experimental treatment is:

    a. the specific setting or combination of factor levels.

    b. a single performance of the experiment.

    c. the relationship between a factor and a response variable.

    d. an independent variable or assignable cause.

4. How many runs are necessary in a full-factorial experiment with five factors, with each factor having two levels?

    a. 25

    b. 32

    c. 2

    d. 10

5. When conducting a DOE, what is the main difference between repetition and replication?

    a. Repetition reflects the sources of variability both within and between runs.

    b. Replication reflects the sources of variability both within and between runs.

   c. Repetition can only be used for fractional factorial designs.

   d. Replication can only be used for fractional factorial designs.

6. When plotting the main effects, a greater slope of the effect indicates:

   a. experimental error.

   b. increased interaction.

   c. confounding.

   d. aliasing.

7. In a resolution IV experiment:

   a. main effects are confounded with other main effects.

   b. main effects are confounded with two-factor interactions.

   c. main effects are not confounded with two-factor interactions.

   d. main effects are confounded with five-factor interactions.

8. If an experimenter wished to have two factors at two levels, and one factor at three levels, which type of experimental design would be appropriate?

   a. Taguchi

   b. Full factorial

   c. Fractional factorial

   d. Mixture

9. An experiment is being conducted to optimize a plastic sealing process. Three factors are believed to influence the sealing process. Each factor has two levels. The experimenter would select what type of design for this experiment?

   a. Latin square

   b. Full factorial

   c. Fractional factorial

   d. Mixture

A three-factor full factorial experiment was conducted. Each factor has two levels. Use the following figure to answer questions 10 and 11.

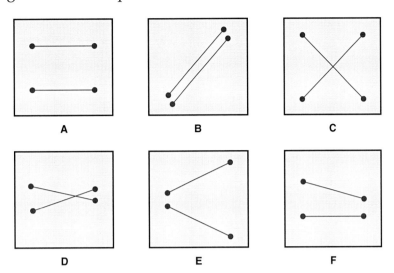

10. Which of the following plots do not indicate the presence of an interaction?

    a. A and B

    b. C and D

    c. E and F

    d. None of these

11. Which of the following plots indicate the most significant interactions?

    a. A and B

    b. B and F

    c. A and F

    d. C and D

12. How many total degrees of freedom are available in the one-way ANOVA summary table?

    a. 10

    b. 14

    c. 24

    d. Not enough information provided

One-Way ANOVA Summary Table					
Source of variation	SS	df	MS	*F* calculated	*F* critical
Between groups	46.8	2	23.4	10.97	3.89
Within groups (error)	25.6	12	2.1		
Total	72.4				

A two-factor full factorial experiment was conducted. Each factor has two levels. Use the following table to answer questions 13 and 14.

Treatment	A Chrome	B Nickel	AB Interaction	Y^1	Y^2	Y^3
1	–	–	+	4.10	4.90	4.30
2	+	–	–	5.50	4.00	4.30
3	–	+	–	9.60	8.70	10.10
4	+	+	+	8.20	7.40	8.70

13. Calculate the absolute effect for factor A (chrome).

    a. 0.60

    b. 0.77

    c. 2.13

    d. 4.67

14. Calculate the absolute effect for the interaction for factor A (chrome) and factor B (nickel).

    a. 0.77

    b. 2.13

    c. 1.77

    d. 4.77

15. Two or more factors that, together, produce a result different than their separate effects is called:

    a. randomization.

    b. orthogonal effects.

    c. replication.

    d. interaction.

16. The *t*-test is used when:

    a. comparing two means.

    b. the distribution is skewed.

    c. the hypothesis is nondirectional.

    d. the hypothesis is omnidirectional.

17. The *F*-test is used when:

    a. the sample size is small.

    b. comparing two variances.

    c. the hypothesis is nondirectional.

    d. there is more than one level.

18. A technique for comparing the *F*-value of the factor/level with an *F*-distribution value is called:

    a. fraction factorials.

    b. orthogonal design.

    c. analysis of variance.

    d. full factorials.

19. If an experiment is balanced, it can also be called a(n):

    a. fraction factorial.

    b. orthogonal design.

    c. analysis of variance.

    d. full factorial.

20. How many treatment conditions are there for seven factors with each factor having three levels?

    a. 4

    b. 10

    c. 343

    d. 2187

21. Orthogonal arrays were first developed by:

    a. Ishikawa.

    b. Fisher.

    c. Deming.

    d. Taguchi.

22. What is a simple method of working with interactions?

    a. Linear graphs

    b. Orthogonal array

    c. Interaction table

    d. Regression

23. Which quality guru developed the *kanban* concept?

    a. Genichi Taguchi

    b. Taiichi Ohno

    c. Masaaki Imai

    d. W. Edwards Deming

24. Using inferior-grade, low-cost components and raw materials in the design process is referred to as:

    a. tolerance design.

    b. parameter design.

    c. Taguchi array.

    d. system design.

25. The concept of the signal-to-noise ratio was developed by:

    a. Ishikawa.

    b. Fischer.

    c. Deming.

    d. Taguchi.

26. The process of selectively upgrading components to eliminate excessive variation is called:

    a. tolerance design.

    b. parameter design.

    c. Taguchi array.

    d. system design.

27. In a pull system, stock is replenished when:

    a. inventory is required.

    b. a kanban is reached.

    c. a shipment is delayed.

    d. the end of the month is reached.

28. In the 5S methodology, the Japanese word for cleaning the work area is:

    a. seiri.

    b. seiton.

    c. seiso.

    d. seiketsu.

Use the following paragraph to answer questions 29–38.

ABC Manufacturing makes U.S. quarter coins by punching the diameter (.955" ± .005") out of a metal sheet and using a gear die to press the reeds on the edges one quarter at a time. It takes one minute per piece to perform the punching step for the diameter, and two minutes per piece to perform the pressing of the reeds step.

29. Creating two holes (one .945" and the other .955") for the quarters to drop through to proceed to the next step would be an example of:

    a. standard work.

    b. a kaizen event.

    c. poka-yoke.

    d. takt time.

30. The time required to complete the punching operation is an example of:

    a. standard time.

    b. cycle time.

    c. takt time.

    d. value-added time.

31. Producing a punch tool that reduces costs and cycle time by creating the reeds at the same time the diameter is being punched is an example of:

    a. standard work.

    b. a kaizen event.

    c. a poka-yoke.

    d. takt time.

32. A customer order for 1000 quarters is due in five days. ABC runs one eight-hour shift per day. What is the takt time?

    a. .417

    b. 2.4

    c. 25

    d. 625

33. A customer order for 1000 quarters is due in five days. ABC runs one eight-hour shift per day. Which of the following is a true statement?

    a. Production will complete the parts on time if no issues occur.

    b. Production will not complete the parts on time.

    c. Production will complete the parts on time if a kaizen event is performed, reducing the cycle time on pressing from 2 minutes to 1.7 minutes if no issues occur.

    d. Production will not complete the parts on time if a kaizen event is performed, reducing the cycle time on pressing from 2 minutes to 1.3 minutes if no issues occur.

34. This type of manufacturing is known as:

    a. lean manufacturing.

    b. design for manufacturing.

c. continuous flow manufacturing.

d. value-added manufacturing.

35. A customer order for 1000 quarters is due in five days. ABC runs one eight-hour shift per day. What lean tool will help with reducing the impact of maintenance on the process?

a. Poka-yoke

b. SMED

c. 5S

d. Standard work

36. A customer order for 1000 quarters is due in 20 days. ABC runs one eight-hour shift per day. Producing only 99 quarters each day is an example of:

a. takt time.

b. heijunka.

c. poka-yoke.

d. standard work.

37. Choosing to reduce the cycle time of the pressing process rather than the punching process is an example of which lean methodology?

a. SMED

b. 5S

c. Theory of constraints

d. Heijunka

38. According to the theory of constraints, when would the attention switch from the pressing process to the punching process?

a. When a kaizen event is completed on the pressing process

b. When a kaizen event is completed on the punching process

c. When pressing throughput > punching throughput

d. When pressing throughput < punching throughput

Use the following paragraph to answer questions 39–42.

A customer order for 1000 quarters is due in five days, which is the maximum amount that the process is designed to run. ABC runs one eight-hour shift per day with one hour for lunch and 15 minutes for maintenance. At the end of five days, 700 good parts and 312 bad parts were produced.

39. The availability is:

   a. .96

   b. .875

   c. .1

   d. .21

40. The performance is:

   a. .9995

   b. .32

   c. .875

   d. 1

41. The quality is:

   a. .70

   b. .69

   c. 1

   d. .21

42. Which of the following is a correct course of action to prepare to complete a similar customer order?

   a. Increase the availability of the process

   b. Increase the quality of the process

   c. Decrease the number of days before the product is due

   d. Increase the performance of the process

Use the following table to answer questions 43–46.

	Weight value	Potential solution			
		A	B	C	D
Implementation cost	0.3	1	3	4	2
Maintenance	0.25	4	2	1	3
Reliability	0.1	4	1	2	3
Loss of customer goodwill	0.35	2.5	2.5	4	1
		2.575	2.375	3.05	2

43. The information in the first column of the ranking matrix is:

    a. solutions.

    b. constraints.

    c. specific criteria.

    d. factors.

44. Which criterion is the most important according to the ranking matrix?

    a. Implementation cost

    b. Loss of customer goodwill

    c. Maintenance

    d. Reliability

45. Which solution is the best according to the ranking matrix?

    a. B

    b. C

    c. A

    d. D

46. The 2.5 in row "Loss of customer goodwill," solutions A and B columns represents:

    a. indecision among the team.

    b. another option to choose such as 1, 2, and so on.

    c. a tie between two solutions.

    d. canceling of the solution from the ranking mathematically.

47. An evaluation method for a set of solutions that involves manufacturing a smaller production run of production-equivalent parts is a:

   a. simulation.

   b. pilot run.

   c. prototype.

   d. model.

48. An evaluation method for a set of solutions that involves using software to evaluate options is a:

   a. pilot run.

   b. simulation.

   c. prototype.

   d. model.

49. An evaluation method for a set of solutions that uses a smaller physical representation of the production part is a:

   a. pilot run.

   b. simulation.

   c. model.

   d. prototype.

50. An evaluation method for a set of solutions that is similar to the production part in form, fit, and function, minus some features is a:

   a. model.

   b. pilot run.

   c. prototype.

   d. simulation.

51. A method for determining the different factors that affect a given decision is:

   a. force-field analysis.

   b. affinity diagrams.

   c. Gantt charts.

   d. root cause analysis.

52. Forces that are for a change or decision are called:

    a. driving forces.

    b. resisting forces.

    c. positive forces.

    d. advocate forces.

53. Forces that are against a change or decision are called:

    a. driving forces.

    b. resisting forces.

    c. positive forces.

    d. advocate forces.

54. Instructions on how to inform the company about an improved process would most likely be found in the:

    a. reaction plan.

    b. communication plan.

    c. mission statement.

    d. quality objectives.

ANSWERS

1. c; Replication reflects the sources of variability both within and between runs and adds degrees of freedom to the experiment. [VII.A.2]

2. d; Randomization is used to assign treatments to experimental units so that each unit has an equal chance of being assigned a particular treatment, thus minimizing the effect of variation from uncontrolled noise factors. [VII.A.2]

3. a; A treatment is the specific setting or combination of factor levels for an experimental unit. [VII.A.1]

4. b; The number of runs required for a full factorial experiment with five factors, with each factor having two levels, is calculated by

$$n = L^F$$

where

n = Number of runs

L = Number of levels

F = Number of factors

$$n = 2^5 = 32$$

[VII.A.1]

5. b; When conducting a DOE, the main difference between repetition and replication is that replication reflects the sources of variability both within and between runs, and repetition is the measurement of a response variable more than once under similar conditions. Repeated measures allow one to determine the inherent variability in the measurement system. [VII.A.2]

6. b; When plotting the main effects, a greater slope of the effect indicates increased interaction. [VII.A.2]

 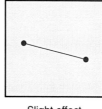 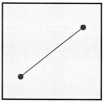

No effect   Slight effect   Significant effect

Factor effect plots

Source: Durivage (2016). Used with permission.

7. c; Resolution refers to the level of confounding in a fractional factorial design. The resolution of a design is generally one more than the smallest-order interaction with which a main effect is confounded.

Experiment resolution		
Resolution	Ability	Example
I	Not useful: an experiment of exactly one run only tests one level of a factor and hence cannot distinguish between the high and low levels of that factor.	2^{1-1} with defining relation I = A
II	Not useful: main effects are confounded with other main effects.	2^{2-1} with defining relation I = AB
III	Estimate main effects, but these may be confounded with two-factor interactions.	2^{3-1} with defining relation I = ABC
IV	Estimate main effects not confounded by two-factor interactions. Estimate two-factor interaction effects, but these may be confounded with other two-factor interactions.	2^{4-1} with defining relation I = ABCD
V	Estimate main effects not confounded by three-factor (or less) interactions. Estimate two-factor interaction effects not confounded by two-factor interactions. Estimate three-factor interaction effects, but these may be confounded with other two-factor interactions.	2^{5-1} with defining relation I = ABCDE
VI	Estimate main effects not confounded by four-factor (or less) interactions. Estimate two-factor interaction effects not confounded by three-factor (or less) interactions. Estimate three-factor interaction effects, but these may be confounded with other three-factor interactions.	2^{6-1} with defining relation I = ABCDEF
VII	Estimates of main factors, two-factor and three-factor effects are not confounded with one another but may be confounded with higher-order interactions. Four-factor and higher interactions may be confounded.	2^{7-1} with defining relation I = ABCDEFG

Source: Adapted from http://en.wikipedia.org/wiki/Fractional_factorial_design.

In a resolution IV experiment, main effects are not confounded by two-factor interactions. [VII.A.2]

8. a; If an experimenter wished to have two factors at one level, and one factor at three levels, a Taguchi design would be the most appropriate choice. There are also some Taguchi designs that combine two-level and three-level factors. [VII.A.3]

9. b; The experimenter would select a full factorial design with an experiment conducted to optimize a plastic sealing process with three factors, with each factor having two levels. This experiment would require eight runs. [VII.A.3]

10. a; Figures A and B do not indicate the presence of an interaction because the lines are parallel.

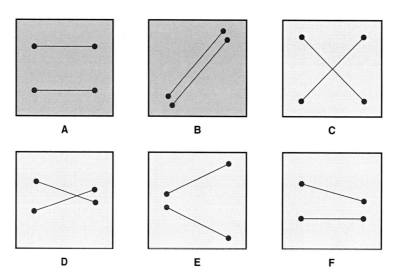

[VII.A.2]

11. d; Figures C and D indicate the most significant interactions because the lines intersect. Figures E and F also indicate the presence of interaction. However, the interaction is not as significant as in Figures C and D.

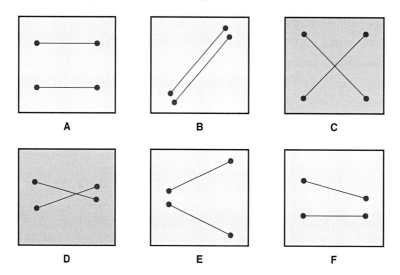

[VII.A.2]

12. b; To calculate the degrees of freedom from the information provided, use

$$df = \frac{SS}{MS}$$

One-Way ANOVA Summary Table					
Source of variation	SS	df	MS	*F* calculated	*F* critical
Between groups	46.8		23.4	10.97	3.89
Within groups (error)	25.6		2.1		
Total	72.4				

Between groups:

$$df = \frac{46.8}{23.4} = 2$$

Within groups (error):

$$df = \frac{25.6}{2.1} = 12$$

Total df = 2 + 12 = 14

Between groups 2, within groups (error) 12, total 14. [VII.A.4]

13. a; A two-factor full factorial experiment was conducted. Each factor has two levels .

Treatment	A Chrome	B Nickel	AB Interaction	Y^1	Y^2	Y^3
1	–	–	+	4.10	4.90	4.30
2	+	–	–	5.50	4.00	4.30
3	–	+	–	9.60	8.70	10.10
4	+	+	+	8.20	7.40	8.70

To calculate the absolute effect for factor A (chrome):

$$E(A) = \left|\bar{Y}_{A+}\right| - \left|\bar{Y}_{A-}\right| = \frac{4.60 + 8.10}{2} - \frac{4.43 + 9.47}{2} = 0.60$$

[VII.A.2]

14. a; A two-factor full factorial experiment was conducted. Each factor has two levels.

Treatment	A Chrome	B Nickel	AB Interaction	Y^1	Y^2	Y^3
1	–	–	+	4.10	4.90	4.30
2	+	–	–	5.50	4.00	4.30
3	–	+	–	9.60	8.70	10.10
4	+	+	+	8.20	7.40	8.70

To calculate the absolute effect for the interaction for factor A (chrome) and factor B (nickel):

$$E(AB) = \left|\overline{Y}_{AB+}\right| - \left|\overline{Y}_{AB-}\right| = \frac{4.43 + 8.10}{2} - \frac{4.60 + 9.47}{2} = 0.77$$

[VII.A.2]

15. d; Interaction is when two or more factors, together, produce a result different than their separate effects. [VII.A.2]

16. a; To compare the means of three or more groups simultaneously, an ANOVA is the most appropriate test. In its simplest form, ANOVA provides a statistical test of whether or not the means of three or more groups are equal, and therefore generalizes the *t*-test to more than two groups. Doing multiple two-sample *t*-tests would result in an increased chance of committing a type I error. For this reason, ANOVAs are useful in comparing three or more means for statistical significance. [VII.A.4]

17. b; An *F*-test is used for the null hypothesis that two normal populations have the same variance. [VII.A.4]

18. c; An ANOVA technique is used to compare the *F*-value of the factor/level with an *F*-distribution value. [VII.A.4]

19. b; A balanced design is a factorial design in which each factor is run the same number of times at the high and low levels. Taguchi orthogonal arrays are balanced to ensure that all levels of all factors are considered equally. [VII.A.2]

20. d; The number of runs required for a full factorial experiment with seven factors, with each factor having three levels, is calculated by

$$n = L^F$$

where

n = Number of runs

L = Number of levels

F = Number of factors

$$n = 3^7 = 2187$$

[VII.A.1]

21. b; Orthogonal arrays were first developed by Ronald A. Fisher in the 1920s and 1930s at Rothamsted Experimental Station. Later in the 1950s Genichi Taguchi further developed orthogonal arrays. [VII.A.1]

22. a; Linear graphs are used to interpret factor interactions. When plotting the main effects, the greater the slope of the effect indicates increased interaction.

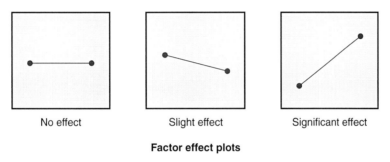

No effect   Slight effect   Significant effect

Factor effect plots

Source: Durivage (2016). Used with permission.

[VII.A.2]

23. b; Taiichi Ohno, an industrial engineer at Toyota, developed kanban to improve manufacturing efficiency. [VII.B.1]

24. b; Parameter design is used to make a product or process more robust to variation over which we have little or no control, using inferior-grade, low-cost components and raw materials in the design process. [VII.A.1]

25. d; Taguchi's signal-to-noise (S/N) ratio outputs are in decibels (dB), or tenths of a bel. One of the advantages of using the dB is that it is a relative unit of measure. [VII.A.1]

26. a; Tolerance design is the process of selectively upgrading components to eliminate excessive variation in order to help keep overall costs low. [VII.A.1]

27. b; A kanban is a system that signals the need to replenish stock or materials or to produce more of an item. Kanban is also known as a "pull" approach. [VII.B.1]

28. b; The 5S elements are:

    • *Sort.* Eliminate whatever is not needed

    • *Straighten.* Organize whatever remains

    • *Shine.* Clean the work area

    • *Standardize.* Schedule regular cleaning and maintenance

    • *Sustain.* Make 5S a way of life

    [VII.B.1]

29. c; Poka-yoke is a term that means to mistake-proof a process by building safeguards into the system that help avoid or immediately find errors. A poka-yoke device is one that prevents incorrect parts from being made, assembled, or stored, or that easily identifies a flaw or error. [VII.B.1]

30. b; Cycle time is the time required to complete one unit from the beginning of the process to the end of the process. [VII.B.2]

31. b; Kaizen is a Japanese term that means gradual unending improvement by doing little things better and setting and achieving increasingly higher standards. [VII.B.3]

32. b; The takt time to produce 1000 quarters due in five days on one eight-hour shift per day is calculated by

$$\text{Takt time} = \frac{\text{Time available}}{\text{Number of units to be produced}}$$

$$= \frac{8 \times 60 \times 5}{100} = 2.4 \text{ minutes per unit}$$

    [VII.B.2]

33. b; The maximum amount of quarters that can be produced in 2400 minutes (5 days × 8 hours/day × 60 min/hour) at 1 quarter/3 min is 800 if no issues occur. Therefore (a) is incorrect. To produce 1000 quarters in 2400 minutes, the cycle time for the system would have to be 2.4 minutes. (c) is incorrect because it is above 2.4 min. (d) is incorrect because the production order would be complete if the cycle time for the pressing operation was reduced to 1.3 min, which would make the cycle time for the system 2.3 min. [VII.B.2]

34. c; Continuous flow manufacturing, commonly referred to as CFM, is a method in which items are produced and moved from one processing step to the next one piece at a time. Each process makes only the one piece that the next process needs, and the transfer batch size is one. CFM is sometimes known as one-piece flow or single-piece flow. [VII.B.2]

35. b; Single-minute exchange of die (SMED) is a system used to reduce changeover time and improve timely response to demand. SMED is a series of techniques pioneered by Shigeo Shingo to facilitate changeovers of production machinery in less than 10 minutes. [VII.B.2]

36. b; Heijunka (production leveling) is a technique for meeting variable customer requirements while reducing variation in the production schedule. It has two forms: volume leveling and product leveling. [VII.B.2]

37. c; The theory of constraints (TOC) is a problem-solving methodology that focuses on the weakest link in a chain of processes. Usually, the constraint is the slowest process. Flow rate through the system cannot increase unless the rate at the constraint increases. [VII.B.4]

38. c; Under the theory of constraints, the process that receives the most attention is the slowest process in the system. Currently, the pressing process is the slowest. When the pressing process becomes faster than the punching process, then the punching process becomes the focus. [VII.B.4]

39. a; Planned production time = (5 days × 8 hours/day × 60 min/hour) – (5 days × 1 hour/day × 60 min/hour) = 2400 – 300 = 2100 minutes.

Actual operating time = 2100 min – (15 min/day × 5 days) = 2100 min – 75 min = 2025 minutes.

$$Availability = \frac{Actual\ operating\ time}{Planned\ production\ time}$$

$$Availability = \frac{2025\ min}{2100\ min} = .96$$

Availability = 2025 min/2100 min = .96

[VII.B.4]

40. a;

$$Performance = \frac{Total\ pieces/Actual\ operating}{Ideal\ run\ time}$$

Total pieces = 1012

Actual operating time = 2025

Ideal run time = .5 parts/min

Performance = 1012/(2025(.5)) = .99

[VII.B.4]

41. b;

$$\text{Quality} = \frac{\text{Number of good pieces}}{\text{Total number of pieces}}$$

Total number of pieces = 1012

Number of good pieces = 700

Quality = 700 ÷ 1012 = .69

[VII.B.4]

42. b; The process is designed to be able to meet the customer order as seen with the high availability (.96) and performance (.9995) numbers. The quality (.69) is the reason why the process is not able to complete the order. [VII.B.4]

43. c;

		Potential solution			
Specific criteria	Weight value	A	B	C	D
Implementation cost	0.3	1	3	4	2
Maintenance	0.25	4	2	1	3
Reliability	0.1	4	1	2	3
Loss of customer goodwill	0.35	2.5	2.5	4	1
		2.575	2.375	3.05	2

In a ranking matrix, the specific criteria by which solutions will be evaluated are placed in the leftmost column. [VII.C]

44. b;

		Potential solution			
Specific criteria	Weight value	A	B	C	D
Implementation cost	0.3	1	3	4	2
Maintenance	0.25	4	2	1	3
Reliability	0.1	4	1	2	3
Loss of customer goodwill	0.35	2.5	2.5	4	1
		2.575	2.375	3.05	2

"Loss of customer goodwill" has the highest associated weight value. [VII.C]

45. b;

		Potential solution			
Specific criteria	Weight value	A	B	C	D
Implementation cost	0.3	1	3	4	2
Maintenance	0.25	4	2	1	3
Reliability	0.1	4	1	2	3
Loss of customer goodwill	0.35	2.5	2.5	4	1
		2.575	2.375	3.05	2

Solution C is the best solution as it has the highest total weighted value. [VII.C]

46. c; A tie in a ranking matrix between two solutions is represented by putting the average of the ratings in both cells:

Tie value = (Rating 1 + Rating 2)/2 = (2 + 3)/2 = 2.5

[VII.C]

47. b; An evaluation method for a set of solutions that involves manufacturing a smaller production run of production-equivalent parts is a pilot run. [VII.C]

48. b; An evaluation method for a set of solutions that involves using software to evaluate options is a simulation. [VII.C]

49. c; An evaluation method for a set of solutions that uses a smaller physical representation of the production part is a model. [VII.C]

50. c; An evaluation method for a set of solutions that is similar to the production part in form, fit, and function, minus some features, is a prototype. [VII.C]

51. a; A method for determining the different factors that affect a given decision is a force-field analysis. [VII.C]

52. a; Forces that are for the change or decision are called *driving forces.* [VII.C]

53. b; Forces that are against the change or decision are called *resisting forces.* [VII.C]

54. b; Instructions on how to inform the company of the improved process would most likely be found in the communication plan. A reaction plan dictates what should be done in the event a step on the control plan is not within the specifications. A mission statement and quality objectives are items that would use the communication plan. [VII.C]

Part VIII

Control

(87 questions)

A. STATISTICAL PROCESS CONTROL (SPC)

1. *Objectives.* Explain the objectives of SPC, including monitoring and controlling process performance, tracking trends, runs, and reducing variation within a process. (Understand)

2. *Selection of variables.* Identify and select critical process characteristics for control chart monitoring. (Apply)

3. *Rational subgrouping.* Define and apply the principle of rational subgrouping. (Apply)

4. *Control chart selection.* Select and use control charts in various situations: $\bar{X} - R$, $\bar{X} - s$, individual and moving range (ImR), p, np, c, u, short-run SPC, and moving average. (Apply)

5. *Control chart analysis.* Interpret control charts and distinguish between common and special causes using rules for determining statistical control. (Analyze)

B. OTHER CONTROLS

1. *Total productive maintenance (TPM).* Define the elements of TPM and describe how it can be used to consistently control the improved process. (Understand)

2. *Visual controls.* Define the elements of visual controls (e.g., pictures of correct procedures, color-coded components, indicator lights), and describe how they can help control the improved process. (Understand)

C. MAINTAIN CONTROLS

1. *Measurement system reanalysis.* Review and evaluate measurement system capability as process capability improves, and ensure that measurement capability is sufficient for its intended use. (Evaluate)

2. *Control plan.* Develop a control plan to maintain the improved process performance, enable continuous improvement, and transfer responsibility from the project team to the process owner. (Apply)

D. SUSTAIN IMPROVEMENTS

1. *Lessons learned.* Document the lessons learned from all phases of a project and identify how improvements can be replicated and applied to other processes in the organization. (Apply)

2. *Documentation.* Develop or modify documents including standard operating procedures (SOPs), work instructions, and control plans to ensure that the improvements are sustained over time. (Apply)

3. *Training for process owners and staff.* Develop and implement training plans to ensure consistent execution of revised process methods and standards to maintain process improvements. (Apply)

4. *Ongoing evaluation.* Identify and apply tools (e.g., control charts, control plans) for ongoing evaluation of the improved process, including monitoring leading indicators, lagging indicators, and additional opportunities for improvement. (Apply)

QUESTIONS

1. Which quality guru is known for developing statistical quality control charts?

    a. Walter A. Shewhart

    b. W. Edwards Deming

    c. Joseph M. Juran

    d. Armand V. Feigenbaum

2. Common cause variation is considered to be the noise of the process. This type of variation is:

    a. highly controllable.

    b. risk-based.

    c. the operator's responsibility.

    d. management's responsibility.

3. Control charts are graphical tools used to monitor a process. Control charts generally do not contain or use:

    a. a centerline.

    b. control limits.

    c. specification limits.

    d. subgroups.

4. A control chart is to be constructed using variables data to monitor a process. The process has an automated vision system to measure the critical feature (height). It has been determined to use a subgroup size of 15. Which of the following control charts is best suited for this application?

    a. $\bar{X}$ and s

    b. XmR

    c. np

    d. g

5. A powder coating line needs to be monitored for quality. A Six Sigma Black Belt has determined to count the number of defects per item using a constant sample size. Which of the following control charts is best suited for this application?

   a. *p*

   b. *np*

   c. *u*

   d. *c*

6. A circuit board manufacturing line requires continuous process monitoring using a count of defective items. Which of the following control charts is best suited for this application?

   a. $\bar{X}$ and *s*

   b. XmR

   c. *u*

   d. *p*

Use the figure below to answer questions 7 and 8.

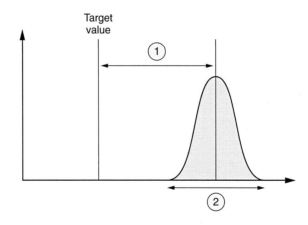

7. The encircled number 1 relates most closely to:

   a. the lower control limit.

   b. the upper control limit.

   c. accuracy.

   d. precision.

8. The encircled number 2 relates most closely to:

   a. the lower control limit.

   b. the upper control limit.

   c. accuracy.

   d. precision.

9. Which of the following subgroup sizes of an $\bar{X}$ and R chart would most likely be used for costly testing?

   a. 1

   b. 2

   c. 3

   d. 4

10. An R chart is used rather than an s chart because it is:

    a. easier to calculate.

    b. more sensitive to variations.

    c. more accurate.

    d. all of these.

11. If only one measurement can be taken at a time, the chart to use is the _____ chart.

    a. trend

    b. median

    c. moving range

    d. sigma

12. Which of the following is the name of an out-of-control pattern?

    a. Unassignable

    b. Causal

    c. All points within $\pm 3\sigma$

    d. Shift or jump

13. A user-friendly chart for the operator is the _____ chart.

    a. moving average

    b. median

    c. trend

    d. cyclical

14. Which of the following subgroup sizes for an $\bar{X}$ and R chart would not be used?

    a. 1

    b. 2

    c. 3

    d. 4

15. An s chart might be used as a measure of dispersion rather than an R chart because it is:

    a. easier to understand.

    b. easier to create.

    c. more accurate.

    d. more sensitive to variations.

16. Those causes of variation that are large in magnitude and are not part of the normal variation are:

    a. assignable causes.

    b. fluctuating causes.

    c. stable causes.

    d. chance causes.

17. Those causes of variation that are small in magnitude are:

    a. special causes.

    b. assignable causes.

    c. chance causes.

    d. fluctuating causes.

18. When interpreting control charts, what are we generally looking for (what do we want to see)?

    a. Randomness

    b. In-control points

    c. Patterns

    d. Randomness and in-control points

19. Calculate the X lower control limit given the following information for an $\bar{X}$ and R chart: $\bar{\bar{X}}$ 904.573, $\bar{R}$ 36.933, n 5.

    a. 883

    b. 904

    c. 926

    d. 987

20. Calculate the X upper control limit given the following information for an $\bar{X}$ and R chart: $\bar{\bar{X}}$ 904.573, $\bar{R}$ 36.933, n 5.

    a. 883

    b. 904

    c. 926

    d. 987

21. Calculate the R lower control limit given the following information for an $\bar{X}$ and R chart: $\bar{\bar{X}}$ 904.573, $\bar{R}$ 36.933, n 5.

    a. 0

    b. 37

    c. 57

    d. 78

22. Calculate the R upper control limit given the following information for an $\bar{X}$ and R chart: $\bar{\bar{X}}$ 904.573, $\bar{R}$ 36.933, n 5.

    a. 0

    b. 37

    c. 57

    d. 78

23. Calculate the estimated sigma given the following information for an $\bar{X}$ and R chart: $\bar{\bar{X}}$ 904.573, $\bar{R}$ 36.933, n 5.

    a. 2.326

    b. 5

    c. 15.878

    d. 36.933

24. Calculate the Cr capability ratio given the following information for an $\bar{X}$ and R chart: $\bar{\bar{X}}$ 904.573, $\bar{R}$ 36.933, n 5, s 15.85, target 900, lower specification limit 850, upper specification limit 950.

    a. 0.951

    b. 1.051

    c. 2.315

    d. 2.798

25. Calculate the C_p capability index given the following information for an $\bar{X}$ and R chart: $\bar{\bar{X}}$ 904.573, $\bar{R}$ 36.933, n 5, s 15.85, target 900, lower specification limit 850, upper specification limit 950.

    a. 0.951

    b. 1.051

    c. 2.315

    d. 2.798

26. Calculate the C_{pk} process capability ratio given the following information for an $\bar{X}$ and R chart: $\bar{\bar{X}}$ 904.573, $\bar{R}$ 36.933, n 5, s 15.85, target 900, lower specification limit 850, upper specification limit 950.

    a. 0.375

    b. 0.567

    c. 0.955

    d. 1.147

27. A run on a control chart refers to:

    a. six consecutive increasing or decreasing points.

    b. a point out of control.

   c. three consecutive points above or below the control limits.

   d. a change in control limits.

28. A *p*-chart is used for:

   a. monitoring the count of nonconformities in a product.

   b. monitoring the fraction nonconforming.

   c. cases where there are few opportunities for nonconformities to occur.

   d. variables data.

29. A fraction nonconforming chart is frequently converted to a percent nonconforming chart:

   a. so that employees can understand it better.

   b. because of the difficulty of variable subgroup size.

   c. so that an average subgroup size (*n*) can be used.

   d. so that the lower control limit will be eliminated.

30. A *u*-chart measures:

   a. the number of nonconforming units.

   b. the count of nonconformities.

   c. the number of standard deviations.

   d. the count of nonconformities/unit.

31. Which of the following is not a purpose of *p*-charts?

   a. To discover the average quality level

   b. Discover low spots that may be due to erratic inspection or superior quality

   c. To suggest places to use $\overline{X}$ and R charts

   d. None of these

32. The problem of variable subgroup size (changing control limits) for a *p*-chart can be minimized by:

   a. using an average subgroup size.

   b. changing the product.

   c. changing the production process.

   d. none of these.

33. When the lower limit of a *c*-chart is less than zero:

    a. change it to 0.

    b. recalculate; an error has been made.

    c. leave it alone.

    d. use a *p*-chart.

34. A *u*-chart measures the:

    a. count of nonconformities/unit.

    b. count of nonconformities.

    c. upper limit.

    d. nonconforming unit.

35. Which of the following concerning the *p*-chart is true?

    a. It applies to quality characteristics that are variables.

    b. It gives a poor overall quality picture.

    c. It can be used for many characteristics.

    d. All of these.

36. An *np*-chart is used for:

    a. controlling the number of nonconformities in a product.

    b. controlling the fraction nonconforming in a lot.

    c. cases where there are few opportunities for a nonconformity to occur.

    d. controlling the number nonconforming of a product.

37. A *c*-chart measures the:

    a. number of nonconforming units.

    b. number of standard deviations.

    c. count of nonconformities.

    d. Poisson factor.

38. The subgroup size of a *u*-chart is:

    a. 1.

    b. variable.

c.   constant.

d.   constant and variable.

39.   Trial control limits are calculated based on at least:

a.   five subgroups.

b.   25 subgroups.

c.   15 subgroups.

d.   35 subgroups.

40.   A *p* control chart would be best to use for which situation described?

a.   You want to chart the fraction of defective printed circuit boards produced each shift. The number of boards produced per shift can vary from 400–500, depending on what type of chip is being manufactured.

b.   You want to chart the average number of flaws per computer produced; random samples of 20–30 computers are checked each hour.

c.   You are tracking the number of defects per washing machine produced.

d.   You want to chart the number of nonconforming light bulbs in a constant sample size of 300 bulbs.

41.   An *np* control chart would be best to use for which situation described?

a.   You want to chart the fraction of defective printed circuit boards produced each shift. The number of boards produced per shift can vary from 400–500, depending on what type of chip is being manufactured.

b.   You want to chart the average number of flaws per computer produced; random samples of 20–30 computers are checked each hour.

c.   You are tracking the number of defects per washing machine produced.

d.   You want to chart the number of nonconforming light bulbs in a constant sample size of 300 bulbs.

42.   A *c* control chart would be best to use for which situation described?

a.   You want to chart the fraction of defective printed circuit boards produced each shift. The number of boards produced per shift can vary from 400–500, depending on what type of chip is being manufactured.

b.   You want to chart the average number of flaws per computer produced; random samples of 20–30 computers are checked each hour.

c. You are tracking the number of defects per washing machine produced.

d. You want to chart the number of nonconforming light bulbs in a constant sample size of 300 bulbs.

43. A *u* control chart would be best to use for which situation described?

a. You want to chart the fraction of defective printed circuit boards produced each shift. The number of boards produced per shift can vary from 400–500, depending on what type of chip is being manufactured.

b. You want to chart the average number of flaws per computer produced; random samples of 20–30 computers are checked each hour.

c. You are tracking the number of defects per washing machine produced.

d. You want to chart the number of nonconforming light bulbs in a constant sample size of 300 bulbs.

44. What is the difference between an attributes chart and a variables chart?

a. Attributes charts are less predictive.

b. Attributes charts provide less statistical data.

c. Attributes charts do not use physical part measurements.

d. All of these.

45. Inconsistent criteria for defective items (that is, different inspectors have different ideas of what a defect is) can lead to:

a. periodic shifts on an attributes chart.

b. a random pattern on an attributes chart.

c. variable control limits on an attributes chart.

d. all of these.

46. How are the control limits for an attributes chart calculated?

a. The centerline value plus or minus three times the approximation of sigma

b. The centerline value plus or minus three times the actual sigma

c. The centerline value plus or minus the range

d. The centerline value plus or minus a percentage of the average value

47. Calculate $\bar{p}$ given the following information for a *p*-chart: sum of *np* 55, sum *n* 2800, *n* 200.

    a. 0

    b. 0.020

    c. 0.125

    d. 0.376

48. Calculate the lower control limit given the following information for a *p*-chart: sum of *np* 55, sum *n* 2800, *n* 200.

    a. –0.01

    b. 0

    c. 0.05

    d. 0.99

49. Calculate the upper control limit given the following information for a *p*-chart: sum of *np* 55, sum *n* 2800, *n* 200.

    a. –0.01

    b. 0

    c. 0.05

    d. 0.99

50. Calculate the estimated sigma given the following information for a *p*-chart: sum of *np* 55, sum *n* 2800, *n* 200.

    a. 0

    b. 0.010

    c. 0.020

    d. Not enough information to calculate

51. Calculate $\overline{np}$ given the following information for an *np*-chart: sum of *np* 55, *k* 14, *n* 200.

    a. 2.438

    b. 2.936

    c. 3.929

    d. 5.791

52. Calculate the process capability given the following information for an *np*-chart: sum of *np* 55, *k* 14, *n* 200, sum of *n* 2800.

    a. 0

    b. 3.929

    c. 5.971

    d. 0.376

53. Calculate the lower control limit given the following information for an *np*-chart: sum of *np* 55, *k* 14, *n* 200, sum of *n* 2800.

    a. −1.959

    b. −1.538

    c. 0

    d. 3.928

54. Calculate the upper control limit given the following information for an *np*-chart: sum of *np* 55, *k* 14, *n* 200, sum of *n* 2800.

    a. −1.959

    b. 3.929

    c. 6.758

    d. 9.816

55. Calculate the estimated sigma given the following information for an *np*-chart: sum of *np* 55, *k* 14, *n* 200.

    a. 0

    b. 1.962

    c. 3.929

    d. Not enough information provided to calculate

56. Calculate $\bar{c}$ given the following information for a *c*-chart: sum of *c* 37, *k* 14.

    a. 0

    b. 1.478

    c. 2.643

    d. 3.769

57. Calculate the lower control limit given the following information for a *c*-chart: sum of *c* 37, *k* 14.

   a. –2.234

   b. 0

   c. 2.716

   d. 3.769

58. Calculate the upper control limit given the following information for a *c*-chart: sum of *c* 37, *k* 14.

   a. 2.234

   b. 2.643

   c. 5.987

   d. 7.520

59. Calculate the estimated sigma given the following information for a *c*-chart: sum of *c* 37, *k* 14.

   a. 1.626

   b. 2.643

   c. 3.259

   d. Not enough information provided to calculate

60. Calculate $\bar{u}$ given the following information for a *u*-chart: sum of *c* 244, sum of *n* 112, *n* 6.

   a. 0

   b. 1.798

   c. 2.179

   d. 3.298

61. Calculate the lower control limit given the following information for a *u*-chart: sum of *c* 244, sum of *n* 112, *n* 6.

   a. –.371

   b. 0

   c. 0.371

   d. 0.478

62. Calculate the upper control limit given the following information for a *u*-chart: sum of *c* 244, sum of *n* 112, *n* 6.

    a. 2.179

    b. 3.798

    c. 3.987

    d. 4.271

63. Calculate the estimated sigma given the following information for a *u*-chart: sum of *c* 244, sum of *n* 112, *n* 6.

    a. 0

    b. 0.603

    c. 1.626

    d. Not enough information provided to calculate

64. The scheduling of maintenance tasks based on operating conditions is referred to as *condition-based maintenance*. Which of the following is an example of condition-based maintenance?

    a. A timing belt that has a high probability of failure at 70,000 miles might be scheduled for replacement at 60,000 miles.

    b. A bearing that usually fails between 1800 and 2600 hours, causing a major shutdown, might be replaced on the weekend after it has had 1500 hours of service.

    c. Spot welding tips must be dressed or changed more frequently when used on galvanized steel.

    d. Performing an oil change every 5000 miles in an automobile.

65. Which of the following best describes the goal of total productive maintenance?

    a. To perform maintenance in a timely manner

    b. To reduce waste from the production line

    c. To ensure that there are no unplanned delays in production

    d. To ensure that proper production planning has occurred prior to the issuing of material

Use the following paragraph to answer questions 66–73 (select the best answer).

A maintenance technician performs the annual maintenance recommended by the manufacturer on a CNC milling machine, which involves changing the belts. The technician also reviews the preventive maintenance checklists and notices that the lubricant level is below the refill line, so the technician fills the tank with more lubricant. The technician also changes the machining tool in the CNC mill since the tool has been used on 200 parts of aluminum. The tool manufacturer indicates that the useful life of the tool is between 250 and 350 parts of aluminum.

66. Changing the belts is an example of:

    a. reliability-based maintenance.

    b. condition-based maintenance.

    c. periodic-based maintenance.

    d. corrective-based maintenance.

67. Refilling the lubricant is an example of:

    a. periodic-based maintenance.

    b. corrective-based maintenance.

    c. reliability-based maintenance.

    d. condition-based maintenance.

68. Changing the tool is an example of:

    a. corrective-based maintenance.

    b. reliability-based maintenance.

    c. condition-based maintenance.

    d. periodic-based maintenance.

69. The preventive maintenance performed by the maintenance technician reduces the:

    a. measurement variation

    b. process variation.

    c. setup time.

    d. infant mortality.

70. The maintenance technician noticed that these $10,000 belts break before the annual maintenance in some years and do not break in other years. The maintenance technician has the options to increase the preventive maintenance cycle from annual to semiannual; to wait until the belt breaks, which will cost $5000 in lost labor and production; to perform a study that will determine a new number other than the 200 parts, which will cost $50,000 every five years; or to wait until the machine operator hears a loud high-pitched sound, which will cost an estimated $6000 per year. The type of maintenance the technician should perform is:

   a. condition-based maintenance.

   b. reliability-based maintenance.

   c. no preventive maintenance.

   d. periodic-based maintenance.

For questions 71 and 72, use the information in question 70 for background.

71. A continuous improvement project began using SPC for the diameter of one of the holes on a part. After several tool change cycles, the continuous improvement team noticed that the SPC chart consistently went out of control at part number 190. Changing the preventive maintenance cycle from 200 parts to being triggered when the SPC chart goes out of control would be an example of the use of:

   a. maintenance analytics.

   b. visual controls.

   c. reliability-based maintenance.

   d. process capability.

72. Of the eight Shewhart rules, which rule would most likely be broken?

   a. Rule 5

   b. Rule 3

   c. Rule 1

   d. Rule 2

73. The refill line on the lubricant container is an example of:

   a. maintenance analytics.

   b. visual controls.

   c. reliability-based maintenance.

   d. process capability.

74. A kaizen event was performed on a process, reducing the process variation from 95% to 60%. The next step the continuous improvement team should implement will be to:

   a. perform another kaizen event.

   b. perform a gage R&R study.

   c. buy a more precise measuring device.

   d. reduce machine downtime.

75. ABC Manufacturing performed a gage R&R study on a pair of calipers used to measure the width of a part. The customer has changed the specifications on the drawing for the width. What part of the gage R&R is expected to have been affected when the gage R&R study is performed?

   a. % study variation

   b. Repeatability

   c. % tolerance variation

   d. Reproducibility

76. A gage R&R study indicates that the number of distinct categories is less than five. Which of the following is a correct next step?

   a. Repeat the gage R&R study using the same samples and operators

   b. Reduce the number of samples

   c. Reduce the number of operators

   d. Identify whether there is a more accurate gage that can be used

77. A torque wrench is verified to be within specifications with a torque analyzer before every use at ABC Manufacturing. ABC wants to move to verifying the torque wrench once a week. The measurement systems analysis evaluation technique that ensures that the torque wrench will exhibit only common cause variation over the week is:

   a. linearity.

   b. stability.

   c. bias.

   d. gage R&R.

78. The primary purpose of the control plan is to:

    a. keep only one item as a variable and maintain all other characteristics as controls per experiment.

    b. implement validations on specific processes.

    c. ensure that process changes are maintained over time.

    d. to create structure for how quality will be implemented throughout the process.

79. Sampling for a process step would most likely be found in which column of the control plan?

    a. Characteristic

    b. Specification

    c. Frequency

    d. Reaction plan

80. What to do when the critical parameter on the control plan goes out of control is indicated on the control plan. It would most likely be found in the _____ column.

    a. reaction plan

    b. characteristic

    c. specification

    d. frequency

81. The requirement for the critical parameter being controlled is indicated in the _____ column.

    a. specification

    b. characteristic

    c. reaction plan

    d. frequency

82. Documentation ensures that:

    a. processes and procedures are maintained over time.

    b. processes and procedures ensure that activities are performed the same way over time.

    c. processes and procedures produce consistent results.

    d. companies will be able to pass their internal and external audits.

83. For documentation to produce consistent results, it must always be coupled with some level of:

    a. skill.

    b. training.

    c. prior knowledge.

    d. certification.

84. A tool used to monitor a process to make sure that the process improvements made are continuing to produce desired results is:

    a. the control plan.

    b. process metrics.

    c. control charts.

    d. gage R&R.

Use the following information to answer questions 85–87.

An audit is being performed, specifically focusing on documentation (SOPs and WIs) and records. The documentation policy requires that the "same function" that originally approved the document must approve changes to documents. The procedure also requires that the documents be available to the employees electronically. The records policy requires the record to be legible, protected from unintended alterations, and with electronic scans acceptable as the permanent record.

During the audit, the auditor observed the following:

SOP 110 Preventive Maintenance—the procedure was originally approved 10/1/2015 by Jane Doe, Maintenance Manager, and Bill Smith, Quality Manager.

SOP 115 Production Control—the procedure was originally approved 11/12/2014 by Todd Jones, Production Manager, and Bill Smith, Quality Manager.

Production Batch Record 1234 was scanned and saved on the company server, which is cloud based. The server requires a unique user name and password for access. The batch was approved for release on 3/14/2016.

85. SOP 110 Preventive Maintenance needs to be updated; however, Jane Doe, Maintenance Manager, was promoted to director of operations, and a replacement was recently hired. Which of the following individual(s) should approve the change to the procedure?

    a. Only the quality manager because he was an original signer

    b. The quality manager and the maintenance manager

    c. The VP of operations and the maintenance manager

    d. The VP of operations, the maintenance manager, and the quality manager

86. SOP 115 Production Control Documentation needs to be updated; however, Todd Jones, Production Manager, is on vacation for six weeks. The production manager directly reports to the VP of operations. Which of the following individual(s) should approve the change to the procedure?

    a. The VP of operations and the quality manager.

    b. The VP of operations and the maintenance manager.

    c. Only the quality manager because he was an original signer.

    d. The procedure should not be changed until production manager Todd Jones returns from vacation.

87. The auditor noticed that Production Batch Record 1234 was approved for release on 3/14/2016, scanned, and saved to the cloud-based server. The auditor asked for the original paper copy. The VP of operations informed the auditor that under the procedure scanned electronic copies are acceptable as the permanent record. Is this a violation of the procedure?

    a. Yes, original paper documents should never be destroyed.

    b. Yes, the cloud-based server is not physically located on the company property.

    c. No, paper copies are required to be saved.

    d. No, the procedure allows electronic scans as the permanent record.

ANSWERS

1. a; Walter A. Shewhart successfully brought together the disciplines of statistics, engineering, and economics and became known as the father of modern quality control. The lasting and tangible evidence of that union, for which he is most widely known, is the control chart, a simple but highly effective tool that represented an initial step toward what Shewhart called "the formulation of a scientific basis for securing economic control." [VIII.A.1]

2. d; *Common causes (variation)* are those that are inherent to the process and generally are not controllable by process operators, and therefore considered to be management responsibility. [VIII.A.1]

3. c; Control charts generally contain a centerline (process average) and upper and lower control limits (±3σ). Specification limits are generally not plotted or recorded on statistical control charts. [VIII.A.1]

4. a; Using variables data with a sample size of 15, an $\bar{X}$ and s chart should be used to monitor the process.

Variables control charts			
Type	**Distribution**	**Sample**	**Application**
$\bar{X}$ and R	Normal	$2 \leq 10$	Measurement subgroups
$\bar{X}$ and s	Normal	> 10	Measurement subgroups

Source: Durivage (2014).

[VIII.A.4]

5. d; A *c*-chart is the most appropriate chart for data that counts the number of defects per item using a constant sample size.

Attributes control charts			
Type	**Distribution**	**Sample**	**Application**
c	Poisson	Constant	Count number of defects per item
u	Poisson	Varies	Count number of defects per item
np	Binomial	Constant	Count of defective items
p	Binomial	Varies	Count of defective items
g	Binomial	Individual	Interval between rare events

Source: Durivage (2014).

[VIII.A.4]

6. d; A *p*-chart is the most appropriate control chart. A circuit board manufacturing line requires continuous process monitoring using a count of defective items.

Attributes control charts			
Type	Distribution	Sample	Application
c	Poisson	Constant	Count number of defects per item
u	Poisson	Varies	Count number of defects per item
np	Binomial	Constant	Count of defective items
p	Binomial	Varies	Count of defective items
g	Binomial	Individual	Interval between rare events

Source: Durivage (2014).

[VIII.A.4]

7. c; Accuracy refers to how closely the values are centered relative to the target/nominal valve. [VIII.A.4]

8. d; *Precision* refers to how closely the values are grouped or clustered together. [VIII.A.4]

9. b; A subgroup size of 2 would be the minimum for use on an $\bar{X}$ and *R* chart used for costly testing. The chart requires a range, so 2 is the minimum. If one sample were used, an individuals and moving range (I-MR) chart would be appropriate. [VIII.A.3]

10. a; An *R* chart is used rather than an *s* chart because it is easier to calculate. An *R* chart is just a simple subtraction of the low value from the high value in a subgroup, whereas an *s* chart requires the calculation of the subgroup's standard deviation. [VIII.A.4]

11. c; When only one measurement can be taken at a time, an individuals and moving range (ImR) chart would be the most appropriate. [VIII.A.4]

12. d; A shift in the process mean has likely occurred when six to nine points in a row are on the same side of the centerline. [VIII.A.5]

13. b; A median chart is user-friendly for the operator as the "middle" value is used and does not require the calculation of the subgroup average. [VIII.A.4]

14. a; A subgroup size of 2 would be the minimum for use on an $\bar{X}$ and *R* chart used for costly testing. The chart requires a range so, 2 is the minimum. If one sample were used, an individuals and moving range (ImR) chart would be appropriate. [VIII.A.3]

15. d; An *s* chart might be used as a measure of dispersion rather than an *R* chart because it is more sensitive to variation. [VIII.A.3]

16. a; Those causes of variation that are large in magnitude and are not part of the normal variation are assignable, or special, causes. [VIII.A.5]

17. c; Those causes of variation that are small in magnitude are chance, or common cause, variation. [VIII.A.5]

18. d; When interpreting control charts, what we are generally looking for (what we want to see) are randomness (we do not want to be able to predict where the next point will fall) and in-control points (all points within the ± sigma control limits). [VIII.A.5]

19. a; To calculate the x lower control limit for an $\bar{X}$ and R chart given $\bar{\bar{X}}$ 904.573, $\bar{R}$ 36.933, n 5, use the following formula:

$$\bar{X}\ LCL = \bar{\bar{X}} - A_2 \times \bar{R}$$

$$X\ LCL = 904.573 - 0.577 \times 36.933 = 883$$

For A_2, see Appendix O, Control Chart Constants, from Durivage (2014). [VIII.A.5]

20. c; To calculate the x upper control limit for an $\bar{X}$ and R chart given $\bar{\bar{X}}$ 904.573, $\bar{R}$ 36.933, n 5, use the following formula:

$$\bar{X}\ UCL = \bar{\bar{X}} + A_2 \times \bar{R}$$

$$X\ UCL = 904.573 + 0.577 \times 36.933 = 926$$

For A_2, see Appendix O, Control Chart Constants, from Durivage (2014). [VIII.A.5]

21. a; To calculate the R lower control limit for an $\bar{X}$ and R chart given $\bar{\bar{X}}$ 904.573, $\bar{R}$ 36.933, n 5, use the following formula:

$$\bar{R}\ LCL = D_3 \times \bar{R}$$

$$R\ LCL = 0 \times 36.933 = 0$$

For D_3, see Appendix O, Control Chart Constants, from Durivage (2014). [VIII.A.5]

22. d; To calculate the R upper control limit for an $\bar{X}$ and R chart given $\bar{\bar{X}}$ 904.573, $\bar{R}$ 36.933, n 5, use the following formula:

$$\bar{R}\ UCL = D_4 \times \bar{R}$$

$$R\ UCL = 2.114 \times 36.933 = 78$$

For A_2, see Appendix O, Control Chart Constants, from Durivage (2014). [VIII.A.5]

23. c; To calculate the estimated standard deviation for an $\bar{X}$ and R chart given $\bar{\bar{X}}$ 904.573, $\bar{R}$ 36.933, n 5, use the following formula:

$$s = \frac{\bar{R}}{d_2} \text{ (Estimate of sigma)}$$

$$s = \frac{36.933}{2.326} = 15.878$$

For A_2, see Appendix O, Control Chart Constants, from Durivage (2014).

Note: Make sure the "d" value is used and not the "D" value. [VIII.A.5]

24. a; Use the following formula to calculate the C_r capability ratio given the following information: $\bar{\bar{X}}$ 904.573, $\bar{R}$ 36.933, n 5, s 15.85, target 900, lower specification limit 850, upper specification limit 950.

$$C_r = \frac{6s}{USL - LSL} = \frac{6 \times 15.85}{950 - 850} = 0.951$$

Since the C_r is less than 1, the process is marginally capable. [VIII.A.1]

25. b; Use the following formula to calculate the C_p capability index given the following information: $\bar{\bar{X}}$ 904.573, $\bar{R}$ 36.933, n 5, s 15.85, target 900, lower specification limit 850, upper specification limit 950.

$$C_p = \frac{USL - LSL}{6s} = \frac{950 - 850}{6 \times 15.85} = 1.051$$

Since the C_p is greater than 1, the process is marginally capable. [VIII.A.1]

26. c; Use the following formula to calculate the C_{pk} process capability ratio given the following information: $\bar{\bar{X}}$ 904.573, $\bar{R}$ 36.933, n 5, s 15.85, target 900, lower specification limit 850, upper specification limit 950.

$$C_{pk} = \text{Minimum of } \frac{\bar{X} - LSL}{3s}, \frac{USL - \bar{X}}{3s}$$

$$= \frac{904.573 - 850}{3 \times 15.85}, \frac{950 - 904.573}{3 \times 15.85} = 1.148, 0.955$$

The C_{pk} is 0.955. Since the C_{pk} is less than 1, the process is not considered to be capable because the process is slightly off center. [VIII.A.1]

27. a; A run on a control chart is six points or more in a row steadily increasing or decreasing. [VIII.A.5]

28. b; A *p*-chart, based on the binomial distribution, is used for the count of defective items when the sample size varies. [VIII.A.4]

29. a; A fraction nonconforming chart (*p*-chart) is frequently converted to a percent nonconforming chart so that employees can understand it better. [VIII.A.4]

30. d; A *u*-chart, based on the Poisson distribution, is used to monitor the count of nonconformities/unit when the sample size varies. [VIII.A.4]

31. d; *p*-charts can be used to discover the average quality level, discover low spots that may be due to erratic inspection or superior quality, and to suggest places to use $\bar{X}$ and *R* charts. [VIII.A.4]

32. a; The problem of variable subgroup (changing control limits) size for a *p*-chart can be minimized by using an average subgroup size to calculate the control limits.

$$p = \frac{np}{n} \text{ (Subgroup)}$$

$$\bar{p} = \frac{\Sigma np}{\Sigma n} \text{ (Centerline)}$$

(Floating control limits)   (Static control limits)

$$\text{UCL} = \bar{p} + 3 \times \sqrt{\bar{p}(1-\bar{p})/n} \qquad \text{UCL} = \bar{p} + 3 \times \sqrt{\bar{p}(1-\bar{p})/(\Sigma n / k)}$$

$$\text{LCL} = \bar{p} - 3 \times \sqrt{\bar{p}(1-\bar{p})/n} \qquad \text{LCL} = \bar{p} - 3 \times \sqrt{\bar{p}(1-\bar{p})/(\Sigma n / k)}$$

(A calculated LCL of less than zero reverts to zero.)

$$s \cong \sqrt{\bar{p}(1-\bar{p})/n} \qquad\qquad s \cong \sqrt{\bar{p}(1-\bar{p})/(\Sigma n / k)}$$

(Estimate of sigma for subgroup)   (Estimate of sigma for chart)

where

    n = Subgroup size

    k = The number of subgroups

[VIII.A.4]

33. a; When calculating the lower control limits for attributes charts (c, u, p, np) if the control limit is negative, the lower control limit becomes zero (0). [VIII.A.4]

34. a; A u-chart, based on the Poisson distribution, monitors the count of nonconformities (defects)/unit and usually uses a variable sample size. Note that a constant sample size may be used. [VIII.A.4]

35. c; A c-chart, based on the Poisson distribution, monitors the count of nonconformities (defects)/unit and usually uses a constant sample size. [VIII.A.4]

36. a; An np-chart, based on the binomial distribution, monitors the count of nonconformities (defects)/unit and usually uses a variable sample size. Note that a constant sample size may be used. [VIII.A.4]

37. c; A c-chart, based on the Poisson distribution, monitors the count of nonconformities (defects)/unit and usually uses a constant sample size. [VIII.A.4]

38. d; A u-chart, based on the Poisson distribution, monitors the count of nonconformities (defects)/unit and usually uses a variable sample size. Note that a constant sample size may be used. [VIII.A.4]

39. b; Trial control limits are calculated based on at least 25 subgroups. [VIII.A.4]

40. a; A p control chart would be best used to chart the fraction of defective printed circuit boards produced each shift. The number of boards produced per shift can vary from 400–500, depending on what type of chip is being manufactured. [VIII.A.4]

41. d; An np control chart would be best used to chart the number of nonconforming light bulbs in a constant sample size of 300 bulbs. [VIII.A.4]

42. c; A c control chart would be best used to chart the number of defects per washing machine produced. [VIII.A.4]

43. b; A u control chart would be best used to chart the average number of flaws per computer produced; random samples of 20–30 computers are checked each hour. [VIII.A.4]

44. d; The difference between an attributes chart and a variables chart is that attributes charts are are less predictive, provide less statistical data, and do not use physical part measurements. [VIII.A.4]

45. d; Inconsistent criteria for defective items (that is, different inspectors have different ideas of what a defect is) can lead to periodic shifts on an attributes chart, random patterns on an attributes chart, and variable control limits on an attributes chart. [VIII.A.4]

46. a; The control limits for an attributes chart calculated using the centerline value plus or minus three times the approximation of sigma. [VIII.A.4]

47. b; Use the following formula to calculate $\bar{p}$ given the following information for a p-chart: sum of np 55, sum n 2800, n 200.

$$\bar{p} = \frac{\Sigma np}{\Sigma n} = \frac{55}{2800} = 0.020$$

[VIII.A.4]

48. b; Use the following formulas to calculate the lower control limit (LCL) given the following information for a p-chart: sum of np 55, sum n 2800, n 200.

$$\bar{p} = \frac{\Sigma np}{\Sigma n} = \frac{55}{2800} = 0.020$$

$$\text{LCL} = \bar{p} - 3 \times \sqrt{\bar{p}(1-\bar{p})/n} = 0.020 - 3 \times \sqrt{0.20(1-0.20)/200} = -0.01$$

Because the calculated value is a negative value, the LCL becomes 0. [VIII.A.4]

49. c; Use the following formulas to calculate the lower control limit (LCL) given the following information for a p-chart: sum of np 55, sum n 2800, n 200.

$$\bar{p} = \frac{\Sigma np}{\Sigma n} = \frac{55}{2800} = 0.020$$

$$\text{UCL} = \bar{p} + 3 \times \sqrt{\bar{p}(1-\bar{p})/n} = 0.020 + 3 \times \sqrt{0.20(1-0.20)/200} = 0.05$$

[VIII.A.4]

50. b; Use the following formulas to calculate the estimated standard deviation given the following information for a p-chart: sum of np 55, sum n 2800, n 200.

$$\bar{p} = \frac{\Sigma np}{\Sigma n} = \frac{55}{2800} = 0.020$$

$$s \cong \sqrt{\bar{p}(1-\bar{p})/n} = \sqrt{0.20(1-0.20)/200} = 0.01$$

[VIII.A.4]

51. c; Use the following formula to calculate $\overline{np}$ given the following information for an *np*-chart: sum of *np* 55, *k* 14, *n* 200.

$$\overline{np} = \frac{\Sigma np}{\Sigma k} \ (\text{Centerline}) = \frac{55}{14} = 3.929$$

[VIII.A.4]

52. b; The process capability for an *np* chart given sum of *np* 55, *k* 14, *n* 200 is simply the process average, which is calculated by

$$\overline{np} = \frac{\Sigma np}{\Sigma k} \ (\text{Centerline}) = \frac{55}{14} = 3.929$$

[VIII.A.4]

53. c; Use the following formulas to calculate the lower control limit (LCL) given the following information for an *np*-chart: sum of *np* 55, *k* 14, *n* 200, and the sum of *n* 2800.

$$\overline{np} = \frac{\Sigma np}{\Sigma k} \ (\text{Centerline}) = \frac{55}{14} = 3.929$$

$$\text{LCL} = \overline{np} - 3 \times \sqrt{\overline{np}\left(1-\left(\Sigma np / \Sigma n\right)\right)} = 3.929 - 3 \times \sqrt{3.929\left(1-\left(55/2800\right)\right)}$$

$$= -1.957$$

Because the calculated value is a negative value, the LCL becomes 0. [VIII.A.4]

54. d; Use the following formulas to calculate the upper control limit (UCL) given the following information for an *np*-chart: sum of *np* 55, *k* 14, *n* 200, and the sum of *n* 2800.

$$\overline{np} = \frac{\Sigma np}{\Sigma k} \ (\text{Centerline}) = \frac{55}{14} = 3.929$$

$$\text{UCL} = \overline{np} + 3 \times \sqrt{\overline{np}\left(1-\left(\Sigma np / \Sigma n\right)\right)} = 3.929 + 3 \times \sqrt{3.929\left(1-\left(55/2800\right)\right)}$$

$$= 9.816$$

[VIII.A.4]

55. b; Use the following formulas to calculate the estimated standard deviation given the following information for an *np*-chart: sum of *np* 55, *k* 14, *n* 200.

$$\overline{np} = \frac{\Sigma np}{\Sigma k} \ (\text{Centerline}) = \frac{55}{14} = 3.929$$

$$s \cong \sqrt{n\overline{p}\left(1-\left(\Sigma np / \Sigma n\right)\right)} = \sqrt{3.929\left(1-(55/2800)\right)} = -1.962$$

[VIII.A.4]

56. c; Use the following formula to calculate $\overline{c}$ given the following information for a *c*-chart: sum of *c* 37, *k* 14.

$$\overline{c} = \frac{\Sigma c}{k} = \frac{37}{14} = 2.643$$

[VIII.A.4]

57. b; Use the following formulas to calculate the lower control limit (LCL) given the following information for a *c*-chart: sum of *c* 37, *k* 14.

$$\overline{c} = \frac{\Sigma c}{k} = \frac{37}{14} = 2.643$$

$$\text{LCL} = \overline{c} - 3 \times \sqrt{\overline{c}} = 2.643 - 3 \times \sqrt{2.643} = -2.234$$

Because the calculated value is a negative value, the LCL becomes 0. [VIII.A.4]

58. d; Use the following formulas to calculate the upper control limit (UCL) given the following information for a *c*-chart: sum of *c* 37, *k* 14.

$$\overline{c} = \frac{\Sigma c}{k} = \frac{37}{14} = 2.643$$

$$\text{UCL} = \overline{c} + 3 \times \sqrt{\overline{c}} = 2.643 + 3 \times \sqrt{2.643} = 7.520$$

[VIII.A.4]

59. a; Use the following formula to calculate the estimated standard deviation given the following information for a *c*-chart: sum of *c* 37, *k* 14.

$$\overline{c} = \frac{\Sigma c}{k} = \frac{37}{14} = 2.643$$

$$s = \sqrt{\overline{c}} = \sqrt{2.643} = 1.626$$

[VIII.A.4]

60. c; Use the following formula to calculate $\bar{u}$ given the following information for a *u*-chart: sum of *c* 244, sum of *n* 112, *n* 6.

$$\bar{u} = \frac{\Sigma c}{\Sigma n} = \frac{244}{112} = 2.179$$

[VIII.A.4]

61. c; Use the following formula to calculate the lower control limit (LCL) given the following information for a *u*-chart: sum of *c* 244, sum of *n* 112, *n* 6.

$$\bar{u} = \frac{\Sigma c}{\Sigma n} = \frac{244}{112} = 2.179$$

$$LCL = \bar{u} - 3 \times \sqrt{\frac{\bar{u}}{n}} = 2.179 - 3 \times \sqrt{\frac{2.179}{6}} = 0.371$$

[VIII.A.4]

62. c; Use the following formula to calculate the upper control limit (UCL) given the following information for a *u*-chart: sum of *c* 244, sum of *n* 112, *n* 6.

$$\bar{u} = \frac{\Sigma c}{\Sigma n} = \frac{244}{112} = 2.179$$

$$UCL = \bar{u} + 3 \times \sqrt{\frac{\bar{u}}{n}} = 2.179 + 3 \times \sqrt{\frac{2.179}{6}} = 3.987$$

[VIII.A.4]

63. b; Use the following formula to calculate the estimated standard deviation given the following information for a *u*-chart: sum of *c* 244, sum of *n* 112, *n* 6.

$$\bar{u} = \frac{\Sigma c}{\Sigma n} = \frac{244}{112} = 2.179$$

$$s \cong \sqrt{\frac{\bar{u}}{n}} = \sqrt{\frac{2.179}{6}} = 0.603$$

[VIII.A.4]

64. c; Condition-based maintenance is the scheduling of maintenance tasks based on operating conditions. Spot welding tips that must be dressed or changed more frequently when used on galvanized steel is an example of condition-based maintenance. [VIII.B.1]

65. c; Total productive maintenance (TPM) is a methodology that works to ensure that every machine in a production process is always able to perform its required tasks so that production is never interrupted. TPM maximizes equipment effectiveness by using a preventive maintenance program throughout the life of the equipment. [VIII.B.1]

66. c; Periodic/preventive maintenance. The scheduling of maintenance tasks based on expected lifetime. Especially useful when multiple items are more efficiently maintained rather than one at a time. Changing the belts annually is an example of periodic/preventive maintenance. [VIII.B.1]

67. d; Condition-based maintenance is the scheduling of maintenance tasks based on operating conditions. Filling the lubricant level when the level is below the refill line is an example of condition-based maintenance. [VIII.B.1]

68. b; Reliability-based maintenance. The scheduling of maintenance based on reliability data, especially if a failure is very costly. Changing the tool is an example of reliability-based maintenance. [VIII.B.1]

69. b; Variation comes from either the measurement or the process. Variation from preventive maintenance is process variation. Setup time and infant mortality may or may not be affected by preventive maintenance depending on the product. [VIII.B.1]

70. c; The technician has several options:

    1. Increase the preventive maintenance to semiannual, which will cost $20,000 annually (periodic-based maintenance).

    2. Wait until the belt breaks, which will cost $5000 annually (no maintenance).

    3. Perform a new study based on their specific product and production for when to implement preventive maintenance, which will cost $50,000 over five years or $10,000 annually. (reliability based maintenance).

    4. Change the belt based on a high-pitched sound prior to belt failure, which will cost $6000 annually (condition-based maintenance).

    The cheapest option is to perform no preventive maintenance. [VIII.B.1]

71. a; Maintenance analytics is the scheduling of maintenance tasks based on data from sensing devices. [VIII.B.1]

72. b; Rule 3, six consecutive points steadily increasing or decreasing, indicating a trend or drift up or down, is the most common type of special cause variation seen on a control chart. A trend may be caused by tool wear, skill improvement, or deteriorating maintenance. [VIII.A.5]

Part VIII
Answers

73. b; Visual controls are approaches and techniques that permit one to visually determine the status of a system, factory, or process at a glance and prevent or minimize process variation. To some degree, it can be viewed as a minor form of mistake-proofing. [VIII.B.2]

74. b; When a process improvement project reduces the part-to-part process variation, a reanalysis of the measurement system should be conducted to determine whether the measurement system is acceptable or needs improvement on the basis of intended use, customer specification, and cost of implementation. [VIII.C.1]

75. c; When a tolerance specification is changed, the % tolerance variation will likely have been impacted. This will require an evaluation or possible re-execution of the gage R&R study. [VIII.C.1]

76. d; The number of distinct categories (NDC) is the number of categories that the measurement system can distinguish, and is directly related to the discrimination of the gage. When NDC is less than 5, a more accurate gage should be used. [VIII.C.1]

77. b; Stability assesses whether the measurement system changes over time. Stability is probably the most important factor and is generally addressed via the calibration program, but other factors such as environmental conditions may cause stability issues. [VIII.C.1]

78. d; A control plan is a living document that identifies critical input and output variables and associated activities that must be performed to maintain control of the variation of processes, products, and services in order to minimize deviation from their preferred values. A control plan is defined as a living document; it is designed to be maintained. [VIII.C.2]

79. c; The control plan should specify a sampling plan that experience has shown to be effective in detecting changes to the process. The plan should identify gages or fixtures to be used. If measurements are to be made, the plan should cross-reference a control plan for monitoring GR&R for the gage involved. [VIII.C.2]

80. a; The control plan should list the steps to be taken when a process change has been detected. This serves as an aid to the responsible personnel during what is often a stressful time. The reaction plan section should cover requirements for containment and inspection of products suspected of having defects. It should also discuss disposition of parts found to be defective. Some control plans prescribe a more intense sampling protocol after certain corrective actions have been taken. [VIII.C.2]

81. a; The specification column contains the requirements and tolerances for the critical parameter being controlled. [VIII.C.2]

82. b; Standard operating procedures (SOPs) and work instructions help reduce process variation and ensure that activities are performed the same way over time. This is especially important when multi-skilled, cross-trained personnel move into a variety of positions. The development and updating of these documents must involve the people who perform the work. [VIII.D.2]

83. b; Training is a critical element for ensuring that the gains of an improved process are maintained. Training is often overlooked or viewed as an unnecessary cost or imposition on the time of already overworked employees. Training employees makes positive contributions toward the ability of the organization to sustain process improvements over the long term. [VIII.D.3]

84. c; Once a process has been improved, it must be monitored to ensure that the gains are maintained and to determine when additional improvements are required. Control charts are used to monitor the stability of the process, determine when a special cause is present, and when to take appropriate action. [VIII.D.4]

85. b; SOP 110 Preventive Maintenance needs to be updated; however, Jane Doe, Maintenance Manager, was promoted to director of operations, and a replacement was recently hired. The procedure was originally approved 10/1/2015 by maintenance manager Jane Doe and Bill Smith, Quality Manager.

    The procedure should be signed by the same function, not necessarily the same individual. Therefore, the maintenance manager and the quality manager should both approve the changes to the procedure. [VIII.D.2]

86. a; SOP 115 Production Control Documentation needs to be updated; However, Todd Jones, Production Manager, is on vacation for six weeks.

    Because the production manager directly reports to the VP of operations, it would be appropriate for the VP of operations and the quality manager to approve the changes to the document. [VIII.D.2]

87. d; The auditor noticed that Production Batch Record 1234 was approved for release on 3/14/2016, scanned, and saved to the cloud-based server. The auditor asked for the original paper copy. The VP of operations informed the auditor that under the procedure, scanned electronic copies are acceptable as the permanent record.

    This would not constitute a violation of the procedure. However, if the scan copy were not legible, it could be a violation of the procedure. [VIII.D.2]

Part VIII
Answers

Part IX

Design for Six Sigma (DFSS) Framework and Methodologies

(23 questions)

A. COMMON DFSS METHODOLOGIES

Identify and describe DMADV (define, measure, analyze, design, and validate) and DMADOV (define, measure, analyze, design, optimize, and validate). (Understand)

B. DESIGN FOR X (DFX)

Describe design constraints, including design for cost, design for manufacturability (producibility), design for test, and design for maintainability. (Understand)

C. ROBUST DESIGNS

Describe the elements of robust product design, tolerance design, and statistical tolerancing. (Understand)

QUESTIONS

1. What are the phases of a design for Six Sigma (DFSS) project?

    a. Define, measure, analyze, improve, control

    b. Plan, do, check, act

    c. Define, measure, analyze, design, verify

    d. Design for Six Sigma

2. Design for Six Sigma (DFSS) is a methodology:

    a. to design parts that result in a six sigma level of quality.

    b. to improve the quality of existing processes to a six sigma level.

    c. to eliminate waste.

    d. to perform kaizen events.

3. Which phase of DMAIC is not present in DFSS methodologies?

    a. Control

    b. Measure

    c. Improve

    d. Analyze

4. Which of the following is not a DFSS methodology?

    a. DMAIC

    b. IDOV

    c. DMADV

    d. DMADOV

5. The *measure* phase in DMEDI is different than DMAIC since:

    a. current performance can be measured in DMEDI.

    b. current performance cannot be measured in DMEDI.

    c. DMAIC uses tools such as quality function deployment.

    d. DMAIC has no baseline to evaluate current performance.

6. The "V" in DMADV stands for a word that means:

    a. to ensure quality is maintained throughout all phases.

    b. to ensure that the design output is capable of meeting its intended use.

    c. to ensure that the design input is capable of meeting its intended use.

    d. to control the change made throughout the phases.

7. Which of the following is a similarity between DMAIC and DMEDI?

    a. Both have a *define* phase

    b. Use of benchmarking to measure current performance

    c. Both have an *explore* phase

    d. Use of simulations to verify design requirements

8. Which is not a common variable for design for X?

    a. Improvement

    b. Cost

    c. Maintainability

    d. Test

9. The X in design for X is:

    a. an industry term for Six Sigma.

    b. a variable that can be any constraint to the design process.

    c. an industry term for manufacturing.

    d. a Japanese symbol for zero defects.

10. A major benefit of design for cost is:

    a. the ability to reduce costs before production and processes are set.

    b. to determine make versus buy decisions.

    c. justification to increase budget.

    d. that costs after production are not considered.

11. The most important contributor to the success of design for producibility, manufacturability, and assembly is:

    a. considering costs in the design process.

    b. having assembly or manufacturing subject matter experts in the design process.

    c. having gates for each phase.

    d. management support.

12. Design for test is unique to other design for X methodologies in the sense that:

    a. parts using design for test are designed to be sampled.

    b. design for test is only used on printed wire boards.

    c. design for test uses one final functional test to verify that a quality part was made.

    d. additional features are added to the design to allow for testing of the product throughout the assembly process.

13. A functional requirement:

    a. dictates how a part should be built.

    b. dictates the performance of a product under specific conditions.

    c. is a requirement that can only be observed but not verified.

    d. is a requirement that requires validation studies to be performed to verify its effectiveness.

Use the following table to answer questions 14 and 15.

A	B	C
$1.0 \pm .5$	$0.5 \pm .2$	$2.0 \pm .3$

14. Calculate the total tolerance of the overall length using the conventional tolerance method.

    a. 2

    b. 2.5

    c. 0.62

    d. 1

15. Calculate the total tolerance of the overall length using the statistical tolerance method.

    a. 2

    b. 2.5

    c. 0.62

    d. 1

16. Taguchi's loss function:

    a. combines cost, target, and variation into one metric.

    b. can only be used for robust designs.

    c. is only concerned with production losses in dollars due to waste of raw material.

    d. None of these.

17. Which of the following is the most common equation of the loss function when using equal bilateral tolerances?

    a. Variance is best

    b. Larger is better

    c. Smaller is better

    d. Nominal is best

18. Designing around the use of inferior-grade, low-cost components and raw materials in the design process is referred to as:

    a. tolerance design.

    b. parameter design.

    c. Taguchi array.

    d. system design.

19. The process of selectively upgrading components to eliminate excessive variation is called:

    a. tolerance design.

    b. parameter design.

    c. Taguchi array.

    d. system design.

20. The output of a Taguchi signal-to-noise (S/N) ratio is in what units?

    a. Percentage

    b. Decibels

    c. Logarithmic

    d. Unit less

21. Determine the signal-to-noise ratio (S/N) for a process that has an average tensile strength of 1200 psi (nominal is best) and a sample standard deviation of 160 psi derived from six samples.

    a. 17.5 dB

    b. 6.16 dB

    c. 7.5 dB

    d. 56.08 dB

22. A part has a specification of 1.000" ± 0.005". The cost to rework a part found to be out of specification is $7.50. Determine the loss function coefficient k.

    a. 1.000

    b. 7.50

    c. 750

    d. 300,000

23. A part has a specification of 1.000" ± 0.005". The cost to rework a part found to be out of specification is $7.50. Determine the loss when the part is produced at 1.004".

    a. $1.00

    b. $4.80

    c. $.05

    d. $7.50

ANSWERS

1. c; Define, measure, analyze, design, validate (DMADV) is a well-recognized design for Six Sigma (DFSS) methodology and an acronym for define–measure–analyze–design–verify. [IX.A]

2. a; Design for Six Sigma (DFSS) provides processes used to engineer and design products with 3.4 defects per million as the goal. [IX.A]

3. a; Define, measure, analyze, design, validate (DMADV), define, measure, analyze, design, optimize, validate (DMADOV), define, measure, explore, develop, implement (DMEDI), and identify, design, optimize, validate (IDOV) design methodologies do not include the *control* phase contained in DMAIC. The control phase is used to monitor the outputs of products and services. [IX.A]

4. a; Define, measure, analyze, design, validate (DMADV), define, measure, analyze, design, optimize, validate (DMADOV), define, measure, explore, develop, implement (DMEDI), and identify, design, optimize, validate (IDOV) are design methodologies and do not include define, measure, analyze, improve, control (DMAIC), specifically the *control* aspect. [IX.A]

5. b; The define, measure, explore, develop, implement (DMEDI) methodology is appropriate where the limitations of define, measure, analyze, improve, control (DMAIC) have been reached and customer requirements or expectations have not been met, or a quantum leap in performance is required. Unlike DMAIC, DMEDI is not suitable for kaizen events, and it is generally more resource intensive, with projects taking considerably longer. [IX.A]

6. b; The "V" in define, measure, analyze, design, validate (DMADV) is for *verify*. This phase is directed at ensuring that the design output meets the design requirements and specifications, and is performed on the final product or process. [IX.A]

7. a; Define, measure, analyze, improve, control (DMAIC) and define, measure, explore, develop, implement (DMEDI) methodologies both utilize a *define* phase. [IX.A]

8. b; Design for X (DFX) would not be appropriate for improvement activities. Define, measure, analyze, improve, control (DMAIC) would be used for improvement activities. [IX.A]

9. a; Design for X is a methodology of using constraints (X) that typically affect the production in the design phase. [IX.B]

10. b; Once a product and the processes that will be used to produce it have been determined, the cost has been largely determined. Trying to make major cost reductions after that point is generally futile. Therefore, significant cost reductions must start in the design stage. [IX.B]

11. b; The best way to make certain that adequate provision for manufacturability and assembly has been made is to have manufacturing/assembly expertise present on the design team. Other strategies to consider:

    1. Minimize part count.

    2. Design parts so they can be used on either side.

    3. Use off-the-shelf parts, standard components, and purchased parts.

    4. Use modular design where possible.

    [IX.B]

12. d; The consideration given during the design stage to improve the testing of a product is called *design for test* (DFT) or *design for testability*. Designs must accommodate an assemble/test/assemble type of production assembly process rather than rely entirely on functional tests of the finished product. [IX.B]

13. b; Functional requirements define how the product is to perform and under what conditions. [IX.C]

14. a; Conventional tolerancing is the traditional way to determine tolerance involving a situation in which several parts are stacked together. To calculate the total tolerance simply add the tolerances:

$$1 + 0.4 + 0.6 = 2.0$$

[IX.C]

15. c; Statistical tolerances are used if the processes producing the lengths of parts (for example) A, B, and C are capable and generate normal distributions; the tolerances on these parts are directly related to the standard deviations. The total tolerance can be calculated by

$$T_{\text{Stack}} = \sqrt{T_A^2 + T_B^2 + T_C^2} = \sqrt{1^2 + 0.4^2 + 0.6^2} = 0.62$$

[IX.C]

16. a; Genichi Taguchi argued that parts near the nominal dimension have more value than others that are within specification but farther away from the nominal value. Taguchi maintained that any deviation from nominal makes the product less valuable. This loss increases as the dimension gets farther

from the nominal or "target" value. The resulting metrics are referred to as *loss functions*. [IX.C]

17. d; Taguchi gives us the loss function concept. The three below are the most commonly used. Nominal is best is the most used loss function as most products produced have a nominal dimension with a ± tolerance. The equations for the three most common loss functions are shown below.

Nominal is best	$L = k(y - \tau)^2$	where $k = A/\Delta^2$
Smaller is better	$L = ky^2$	where $k = A/y^2$
Larger is better	$L = k(1/y^2)$	where $k = Ay^2$

where

   L = Cost incurred when quality deviates from the target

   y = Measured value

   τ = Target/nominal value

   k = Quality loss coefficient

   A = Cost to repair or replace

   Δ^2 = (½ of the total tolerance)

[IX.C]

18. b; Parameter design is used to make a product or process more robust to variation over which we have little or no control when using inferior-grade, low-cost components and raw materials in the design process. [IX.C]

19. a; Tolerance design is the process of selectively upgrading components to eliminate excessive variation to help keep overall costs low. [IX.C]

20. b; Taguchi's signal-to-noise (S/N) ratio outputs are in decibels (dB), or tenths of a bel. One of the advantages of using dB is that it is a relative unit of measure. [IX.C]

21. a; A process that has an average tensile strength of 1200 psi (nominal is best) and a sample standard deviation of 160 psi derived from six samples. Calculate the signal-to-noise S/N_N ratio for nominal is best.

   The signal to noise S/N_N ratio for nominal is best is calculated by

$$S/N_N = 10\log_{10}\left[\left(\frac{\bar{y}^2}{s^2}\right) - \left(\frac{1}{n}\right)\right]$$

where

$\bar{y}$ = Process average

s = Standard deviation

n = Sample size

$$S/N_N = 10\log_{10}\left[\left(\frac{\bar{y}^2}{s^2}\right)-\left(\frac{1}{n}\right)\right] = 10\log_{10}\left[\left(\frac{1200^2}{160^2}\right)-\left(\frac{1}{6}\right)\right] = 17.5\text{dB}$$

[IX.C]

22. d; To determine the loss function coefficient k for a part that has a specification of 1.000" ± 0.005", with the cost to rework a part found to be out of specification of $7.50, use the following formula:

$$k = A/\Delta^2$$

where

A = Cost to repair or replace

Δ^2 = (½ of the total tolerance)

$k = A/\Delta^2 = 7.50/.005^2 = 300{,}000$

The quality loss coefficient is 300,000. [IX.C]

23. b; Determine the loss when a part is produced at 1.004" that has a specification of 1.000" ± 0.005" with the cost to rework a part found to be out of specification of $7.50 ($k$ = 300,000). To calculate cost incurred when quality deviates from the target, use the following formula:

$$L = k(y - t)^2$$

where

L = Cost incurred when quality deviates from the target

y = Measured value

t = Target/nominal value

k = Quality loss coefficient

$$L = k(y - t)^2 = 300{,}000(1.004 - 1.000)^2 = 4.80$$

The cost incurred when quality deviates from the target (part produced at 1.004) is $4.80. [IX.C]

Section 2

Practice Test

(150 questions)

QUESTIONS

1. A Master Black Belt is usually associated with an individual who:

   a. is typically assigned full-time to train, mentor, and lead improvement projects.

   b. is typically assigned full-time to train, mentor, and lead the strategy for chartering an organization's strategic projects.

   c. retains their regular position, but is trained in the tools, methods, and skills necessary to conduct Six Sigma improvement projects.

   d. has the authority or ability to make changes in the process as required.

2. The type of training when a less experienced employee receives guidance from an experienced employee that may or may not be part of management is called:

   a. mentoring/coaching.

   b. motivational.

   c. inspirational.

   d. self-directed.

3. This is the role in the RACI model where the decision must be discussed with the individual before a decision is made.

   a. Accountable

   b. Consulted

   c. Informed

   d. Responsible

4. What is the relationship between a process and a system?

   a. Systems are a series of interrelated processes

   b. Processes are system outputs

   c. Processes are a series of interrelated systems

   d. Systems are process inputs

5. Brainstorming is most associated with:

   a. eliminating ideas.

   b. reducing ideas.

   c. generating ideas.

   d. ranking ideas.

6. The lack of symmetry of data is called:

   a. skewness.

   b. leptosis.

   c. modality.

   d. kurtosis.

7. A tool used to show the activities and sub-activities necessary to complete a goal is a(n):

   a. Gantt chart.

   b. interrelationship diagram.

   c. work breakdown structure.

   d. tree diagram.

8. A formal or informal communication used to acknowledge a key milestone is:

   a. a newsletter.

   b. an annual report.

   c. gossip.

   d. an announcement.

9. In an activity network diagram, the _____ determine(s) the minimal length of the entire project.

   a. critical path

   b. nodes

   c. slack times

   d. levels

10. Organizations usually utilize benchmarking to:

    a. increase market penetration.

    b. collect and develop data on industry best practices.

    c. perform root cause analysis.

    d. determine critical-to-quality features.

11. The terms "training" and "education" are often used interchangeably. However, training is best described as:

    a. increasing an understanding of concepts.

    b. preparation for future opportunities.

    c. skill-based instruction.

    d. knowledge-based instruction.

12. According to Williams (2008), the four components of any project are scope, quality, time, and:

    a. constraints.

    b. cost.

    c. schedule.

    d. boundaries.

13. ABC Manufacturing performed a gage R&R study on a pair of calipers for width of a part. The customer has changed the specifications on the drawing for the width. What part of the gage R&R is expected to have been affected when the gage R&R study is performed?

    a. % tolerance variation

    b. Repeatability

c. Reproducibility

d. % study variation

14. A Black Belt is usually associated with an individual who:

    a. retains their regular position, but is trained in the tools, methods, and skills necessary to conduct Six Sigma improvement projects.

    b. has the authority or ability to make changes in the process as required.

    c. is typically assigned full-time to train, mentor, and lead the strategy for chartering an organization's strategic projects.

    d. is typically assigned full-time to train, mentor, and lead improvement projects.

15. The most important contributor to the success of design for producibility, manufacturability, and assembly is:

    a. management support.

    b. considering costs in the design process.

    c. having assembly or manufacturing subject matter experts involved in the design process.

    d. having gates for each phase.

16. Lean Six Sigma:

    a. is a management concept that helps managers at all levels monitor results.

    b. was developed by the Toyota Motor Company.

    c. was established by the U.S. Congress in 1987 to raise awareness of quality management.

    d. combines the individual concepts of lean and Six Sigma.

17. What are the phases of a design for Six Sigma (DFSS) project?

    a. Define, measure, analyze, design, verify

    b. Design for Six Sigma

    c. Define, measure, analyze, improve, control

    d. Plan, do, check, act

18. As parts are made, they are placed in trays that hold 30 parts. If a tray contains six defective parts and you sample one part from the tray, what is the probability that it will be a defective part?

    a. 30%

    b. 80%

    c. 6%

    d. 20%

19. Any individual or group with an interest in the business is considered a(an):

    a. regulator.

    b. stakeholders.

    c. shareholders.

    d. employee.

20. A technique for the generation of ideas where ideas are written down without any discussion, after which the ideas are ranked is:

    a. nominal group technique.

    b. configuration management.

    c. brainstorming.

    d. affinity analysis.

21. The peakedness of the data is called:

    a. modal.

    b. kurtosis.

    c. skewness.

    d. leptosis.

22. When team members begin to understand the need to operate as a team rather than as a group of individuals, this is referred to as:

    a. norming.

    b. storming.

    c. performing.

    d. forming.

Use the following information to answer questions 23–25.

An audit is being performed, specifically focusing on documentation (SOPs and WIs) and records. The documentation policy requires that the "same function" must approve changes to documents that originally approved the document. The procedure also requires that the documents be available to the employees electronically. The records policy requires the record to be legible, protected from unintended alterations, and with electronic scans acceptable as the permanent record.

During the audit, the auditor observed the following:

SOP 110 Preventive Maintenance—the procedure was originally approved 10/1/2015 by Jane Doe, Maintenance Manager, and Bill Smith, Quality Manager.

SOP 115 Production Control—the procedure was originally approved 11/12/2014 by Todd Jones, Production Manager, and Bill Smith, Quality Manager.

Production Batch Record 1234 was scanned and saved on the company server, which is cloud based. The server requires a unique user name and password for access. The batch was approved for release on 3/14/2016.

23. SOP 115 Production Control Documentation needs to be updated; however, production manager Todd Jones, is on vacation for 6 weeks. The production manager directly reports to the VP of operations. Which of the following individual(s) should approve the change to the procedure?

   a. The procedure should not be changed until production manager Todd Jones returns from vacation.

   b. The VP of operations and the quality manager.

   c. The VP of operations and the maintenance manager.

   d. Only the quality manager because he was an original signer.

24. The auditor noticed that Production Batch Record 1234 was approved for release on 3/14/2016, scanned, and saved to the cloud-based server. The auditor asked for the original paper copy. The VP of operations informed the auditor that under the procedure scanned electronic copies are acceptable as the permanent record. Is this a violation of the procedure?

   a. No, the procedure allows electronic scans as the permanent record.

   b. Yes, original paper documents should never be destroyed.

   c. Yes, the cloud-based server is not physically located on the company property.

   d. No, paper copies are required to be saved.

25. SOP 110 Preventive Maintenance needs to be updated; however, maintenance manager Jane Doe, was promoted to director of operations, and a replacement was recently hired. Which of the following individual(s) should approve the change to the procedure?

   a. The quality manager and the maintenance manager

   b. The VP of operations and the maintenance manager

   d. Only the quality manager because he was an original signer

   c. The VP of operations, the maintenance manager, and quality manager

26. In the Kano model, expected requirements are those that will cause:

   a. high customer dissatisfaction if not met and high customer satisfaction if met.

   b. low customer dissatisfaction if not met but high customer satisfaction if met.

   c. low customer dissatisfaction if not met and low customer satisfaction if met.

   d. high customer dissatisfaction if not met but low customer satisfaction if met.

27. The benchmarking process can be ineffective if the process:

   a. is not industry specific.

   b. was provided by a consultant.

   c. has not been fully defined.

   d. is fully mapped.

28. The time required to complete one unit from the beginning of the process to the end of the process is defined as the:

   a. takt time.

   b. throughput.

   c. touch time.

   d. cycle time.

29. Calculate the variance given the sample set of data 45, 51, 46, 53, 46, 57, 51, 72, 55, 61.

    a. 67.79

    b. 2.15

    c. 8.23

    d. 53.70

30. A cross-divisional Six Sigma improvement team from different locations that may not meet in person is a(n):

    a. informal team.

    b. formal team.

    c. virtual team.

    d. ineffective team.

31. Quality planning, quality control, and quality improvement are part of:

    a. F. M. Gryna's quality trilogy.

    b. W. Edwards Deming's 14 points.

    c. W. Edwards Deming's seven deadly sins of quality.

    d. Joseph M. Juran's quality trilogy.

32. A functional requirement:

    a. dictates the performance of a product under specific conditions.

    b. can only be observed but not verified.

    c. requires validation studies to be performed to verify its effectiveness.

    d. dictates how a part should be built.

33. With n observations selected from a random sample, each of which could be classified into exactly one of K categories, how many degrees of freedom does a goodness-of-fit test with specified probabilities have?

    a. $K + 1$

    b. $K - 1$

    c. K

    d. $K - 2$

34. Which of the following is the least effective way to measure customer loyalty?

    a. Customer retention rate

    b. Quarterly sales volume

    c. Customer abandonment rate

    d. Customer referrals

35. What type of error is rejecting the null hypothesis when the null hypothesis is true?

    a. Type I

    b. Type III

    c. Type IV

    d. Type II

36. Supporting, opposing, helping, and hindering are:

    a. types of stakeholders.

    b. four features that affect stakeholders.

    c. analysis planning steps.

    d. four steps of stakeholder analysis.

37. This individual does not generally attend regular Six Sigma project team meetings.

    a. Team leader

    b. Facilitator

    c. Champion

    d. Coach

38. Taguchi's loss function:

    a. is only concerned with production losses in dollars due to waste of raw material.

    b. combines cost, target, and variation into one metric.

    c. can only be used for robust designs.

    d. None of these.

39. A process improvement team has just made a significant breakthrough. The plant manager formally recognizes the achievement during an all-employee meeting. This is an example of:

    a. individual performance.

    b. rewards.

    c. product realization.

    d. recognition.

40. Which quality guru is known as the "father" of statistical quality control?

    a. Walter A. Shewhart

    b. Armand V. Feigenbaum

    c. W. Edwards Deming

    d. Joseph M. Juran

41. When a team member decides not to express their opinion because they are fearful of alienating others in the group, this is known as:

    a. invulnerability.

    b. groupthink.

    c. confirmation.

    d. brainstorming.

42. The voice of the customer is:

    a. an expression of customer wants.

    b. the communication method used for network marketing.

    c. a measure of the capability of a process.

    d. the response heard from market promotions.

43. The tool that can be used to organize the ideas developed during a brainstorming session into larger categories is the:

    a. Gantt chart.

    b. affinity diagram.

    c. work breakdown structure.

    d. interrelationship diagram.

44. When a Six Sigma process improvement team has pooled their collective expertise to develop a solution, this is referred to as:

    a. groupthink.

    b. action items.

    c. decision making.

    d. coordination.

45. Calculate the C_{pk} process capability ratio given the following information: $\bar{\bar{X}}$ 904.573, $\bar{R}$ 36.933, n 5, s 15.85, target 900, lower specification limit 850, upper specification limit 950.

    a. 0.567

    b. 0.955

    c. 0.375

    d. 1.147

46. A process has a mean of 53.7 and sigma of 8.23. What percentage of product generated will be greater than 60?

    a. 25%

    b. 78%

    c. 22%

    d. 75%

47. The _____ is often the best person able to break roadblocks when implementing change.

    a. champion

    b. Master Black Belt

    c. Black Belt

    d. manager

48. _____ training is based on the demonstration of measurable outcomes.

    a. Formal

    b. Informal

    c. Self-paced

    d. Competency

49. An organization wishes to provide training to improve employee morale. The first step in developing a training program is:

    a. assessing the need for the training.

    b. hiring a certified trainer.

    c. designing a training plan.

    d. developing the curriculum.

50. Which of the following components of a measurement system is associated with different operators and different gages?

    a. Bias

    b. Reproducibility

    c. Stability

    d. Linearity

51. Specifications most accurately represent:

    a. the voice of the customer.

    b. quality function deployment.

    c. critical-to-quality attributes.

    d. process limits.

Use the following paragraph to answer questions 52–57.

ABC Manufacturing makes U.S. quarter coins by punching the diameter (.955" ± .005") out of a metal sheet and using a gear die to press the reeds on the edges one quarter at a time. It takes one minute per piece to perform the punching step for the diameter, and two minutes per piece to perform the pressing of the reeds step.

52. A customer order for 1000 quarters is due in five days. ABC runs one eight-hour shift per day. What is the takt time?

    a. 25

    b. 625

    c. .417

    d. 2.4

53. According to the theory of constraints, when would the attention switch from the pressing process to the punching process?

    a. When pressing throughput < punching throughput

    b. When a kaizen event is completed on the pressing process

    c. When a kaizen event is completed on the punching process

    d. When pressing throughput > punching throughput

54. Choosing to reduce the cycle time of the pressing process rather than the punching process is an example of which lean methodology?

    a. Theory of constraints

    b. Heijunka

    c. SMED

    d. 5S

55. Creating two holes (one .945" and the other .955") for the quarters to drop through to proceed to the next step would be an example of:

    a. poka-yoke.

    b. takt time.

    c. standard work.

    d. a kaizen event.

56. This type of manufacturing is known as:

    a. value-added manufacturing.

    b. lean manufacturing.

    c. design for manufacturing.

    d. continuous flow manufacturing.

57. Producing a punch tool that reduces the costs and cycle time by creating the reeds at the same time the diameter is being punched is an example of:

    a. standard work.

    b. a kaizen event.

    c. poka-yoke.

    d. takt time.

58. The X in "critical to X" stands for:

    a. any constraints from production that need to be included in the design phase.

    b. quality.

    c. any variable that impacts the customer.

    d. cost.

59. Which of the following is a similarity between DMAIC and DMEDI?

    a. Use of benchmarking to measure current performance

    b. Use of simulations to verify design requirements

    c. Both have an *explore* phase

    d. Both have a *define* phase

60. This type of data is classified into categories with no order implied.

    a. Nominal

    b. Ordinal

    c. Interval

    d. Ratio

61. _____ help(s) manage the project by indicating the relative success of the project.

    a. Project goals

    b. Project plan

    c. Project performance measurement

    d. Project scope

62. The rate in time per unit at which the process must complete units to achieve the customer demand is defined as the:

    a. cycle time.

    b. takt time.

    c. touch time.

    d. throughput.

63. Calculate the precision-to-tolerance ratio (PTR) using the following information:

    Lower specification limit –150

    Upper specification limit 150

    σ_{MS} 8.45

    a. 28.1%

    b. 32.7%

    c. 41.3%

    d. 16.9%

64. This role in the RACI model is where the individual is ultimately held responsible for results.

    a. Consulted

    b. Informed

    c. Responsible

    d. Accountable

65. A Green Belt is usually associated with an individual who:

    a. is typically assigned full-time to train, mentor, and lead improvement projects.

    b. has the authority or ability to make changes in the process as required.

    c. retains their regular position, but is trained in the tools, methods, and skills necessary to conduct Six Sigma improvement projects.

    d. is typically assigned full-time to train, mentor, and lead the strategy for chartering organization's strategic projects.

66. Work breakdown structures serve as inputs into tools such as:

    a. FMEA.

    b. control plan.

    c. affinity diagram.

    d. Gantt chart.

67. To ensure that all the activities for a particular stage in a process are completed before moving to the next stage, _____ are needed.

   a. Gantt charts

   b. interrelationship diagrams.

   c. tollgate reviews.

   d. work breakdown structures.

68. For the normal curve, approximately 68% of the data will fall between:

   a. ±2σ.

   b. ±3σ.

   c. ±1σ.

   d. ±5σ.

69. The tool that captures requirements on inputs into and outputs from a process is:

   a. requirements tree analysis.

   b. SIPOC.

   c. quality function deployment.

   d. Kano model.

70. An organization chart is an example of a:

   a. Gantt chart.

   b. work breakdown structure.

   c. tree diagram.

   d. interrelationship diagram.

71. Which phase of DMAIC is not present in DFSS methodologies?

   a. Analyze

   b. Control

   c. Measure

   d. Improve

72. A customer requires 116 units per day. The plant operates one eight-hour shift. What is the required takt time?

    a. 4.14

    b. 8

    c. 14.5

    d. 116

73. The project management tool that allows you to see planned and completed tasks on a timeline is the:

    a. interrelationship diagram.

    b. Gantt chart.

    c. affinity diagram.

    d. tree diagram.

74. A measurement system has been evaluated, with the following results: repeatability 0.13% and reproducibility 10.38%. What is the gage R&R?

    a. 1.35%

    b. 10.25%

    c. 10.38%

    d. 0.13%

75. A project scope will mostly likely cause a project to fail if which of the following is true?

    a. The scope is too broad.

    b. The scope is too short.

    c. The scope is qualitative.

    d. The scope is too long.

76. The project scope ensures that:

    a. the purpose of the project is clear.

    b. the root cause is identified.

    c. costs of the project are identified.

    d. the constraints of the project are clear.

77. The team phase where team members understand one another and recognize each other's strengths and weaknesses is referred to as:

    a. norming.

    b. performing.

    c. storming.

    d. forming.

78. This type of data has meaningful differences, and an absolute zero exists.

    a. Ordinal

    b. Nominal

    c. Interval

    d. Ratio

79. Which model of the following is the best model for identifying stakeholders in a proposed change in a manufacturing process?

    a. SIPOC

    b. DMAIC

    c. DFSS

    d. PDCA

80. The material that has been input into the process but that has not reached the output or finished stage can be defined as:

    a. takt time.

    b. work in progress (WIP).

    c. work in queue (WIQ).

    d. touch time.

81. The team phase where team members struggle to understand the team goal and its meaning for them individually is referred to as:

    a. storming.

    b. norming.

    c. forming.

    d. performing.

82. A powder coating operation is being monitored. Which of the following is not considered discrete data?

    a. Errors in the batch record

    b. Pass/fail color sheen test

    c. Go/no-go measurements

    d. Number of nonconforming parts

83. A tool used to choose between several scenarios of unequal value is called a:

    a. work breakdown structure.

    b. relationship matrix.

    c. prioritization matrix.

    d. interrelationship diagram.

84. Calculate the standard error given the following sample set of data: 43, 45, 40, 39, 42, 44, 41.

    a. 8.23

    b. 1.23

    c. 1.54

    d. 1.77

85. A project team has discussed several possible solutions based on data provided by the process owner. The team has reached agreement on the course of action. This agreement is called:

    a. purpose.

    b. planning.

    c. consensus.

    d. agenda.

86. A good Six Sigma project team member is characterized by:

    a. being on time.

    b. fostering concurrent discussions.

    c. being politically correct.

    d. avoiding constructive debate.

87. The costs associated with acceptance sampling are:

    a. external failure costs.

    b. internal failure costs.

    c. appraisal costs.

    d. prevention costs.

88. Determine the signal-to-noise (S/N) ratio for a process that has an average tensile strength of 1200 psi (nominal is best) and a sample standard deviation of 160 psi derived from six samples.

    a. 7.5 dB

    b. 56.08 dB

    c. 17.5 dB

    d. 6.16 dB

89. Benchmarking is defined as:

    a. self-improvement study groups composed of a small number of employees.

    b. an improvement process in which a company measures its performance against that of best-in-class companies and processes.

    c. a breakthrough approach involving the restructuring of an entire organization and its processes.

    d. the application of statistical techniques to control a process.

90. When the word "or" is verbalized in probability, it means to perform the arithmetic operation of:

    a. addition.

    b. exponentiation.

    c. multiplication.

    d. division.

Use the table below to answer questions 91–92.

Time	Strength				
X	Y	XY	X^2	Y^2	
1.0	41	41	1.0	1681	
1.5	41	61.5	2.3	1681	
2.0	41	82	4.0	1681	
2.5	43	107.5	6.3	1849	
3.0	43	129	9.0	1849	
3.5	44	154	12.3	1936	
4.0	50	200	16.0	2500	
17.5	**303.0**	**775.0**	**50.8**	**13177.0**	**Sum**

91. What is the coefficient of determination?

    a. 1.000

    b. 0.843

    c. 17.50

    d. 0.710

92. What is the correlation coefficient?

    a. 0.710

    b. 0.843

    c. 1.000

    d. 17.50

93. A process improvement team has completed a PFMEA. Which of the following tools would best be suited to help the team focus their efforts based on the PFMEA?

    a. Pareto analysis

    b. Force-field analysis

    c. SWOT analysis

    d. Statistical analysis

94. In five years, $5000 will be available. What is the net present value (NPV) of that money, assuming an annual interest rate of 10%?

   a. $1581.14

   b. $3104.61

   c. $500.00

   d. $5000.00

95. Which of the following cases would be considered the most desirable in terms of the relationship of the specification to the process spread?

   a. $6\sigma > \text{USL} - \text{LSL}$

   b. $6\sigma = \text{USL} - \text{LSL}$

   c. $3\sigma = \text{USL}$

   d. $6\sigma < \text{USL} - \text{LSL}$

96. If the mean of a sample drawn from a population is 2.15 and the population standard deviation is known to be 0.8, calculate the 95% confidence interval for the average if the sample size is 75.

   a. 1.996 to 2.427

   b. 1.969 to 2.331

   c. 1.960 to 2.333

   d. 1.979 to 2.341

97. A process has a mean of 53.7 and sigma of 8.23. What value (x) for the lower specification limit will yield 5% scrap?

   a. 60

   b. 50

   c. 30

   d. 40

98. The numerator of the capability index equation is the:

   a. process spread.

   b. standard error.

   c. tolerance.

   d. capability ratio.

Use the following figure to answer questions 99–100.

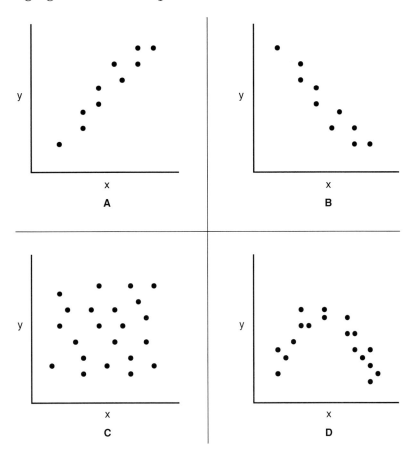

99. Which figure demonstrates positive correlation?

    a. Figure D

    b. Figure C

    c. Figure B

    d. Figure A

100. Which figure demonstrates perfect negative correlation?

    a. Figure C

    b. Figure A

    c. Figure B

    d. Figure D

101. Two or more factors that, together, produce a result different than their separate effects is called:

    a. orthogonal effects.

    b. replication.

    c. interaction.

    d. randomization.

102. Calculate the process capability given the following information for an *np* chart: sum of *np* 55, *k* 14, *n* 200.

    a. 0.020

    b. 0

    c. 4.133

    d. 3.929

103. The likelihood that current controls will prevent a failure from reaching the customer is addressed by:

    a. severity.

    b. FMEA.

    c. detection.

    d. occurrence.

104. In a pull system, stock is replenished when:

    a. a kanban is reached.

    b. a shipment is delayed.

    c. the end of the month is reached.

    d. inventory is required.

105. Sampling for a process step would most likely be found in which column of the control plan?

    a. Frequency

    b. Reaction plan

    c. Characteristic

    d. Specification

Use the following diagram to answer questions 106–108.

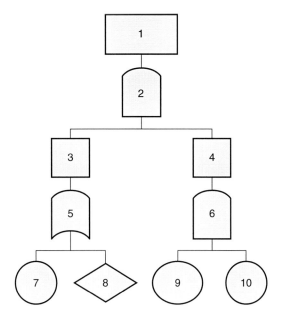

106. Which of the fault tree analysis (FTA) symbols indicates the primary event?

    a. 3

    b. 4

    c. 1

    d. 3 and 4

107. Which of the FTA symbols indicates an AND gate?

    a. 6

    b. 2 and 6

    c. 2

    d. 5

108. Which of the FTA symbols indicates an OR gate?

    a. 6

    b. 5 and 6

    c. 2

    d. 5

109. When constructing a Pareto diagram, where is the "other" category placed?

    a. Last column

    b. First column

    c. The "other" column should not be used

    d. Depends on the number of other items

110. What type of error is failing to reject the null hypothesis when the null hypothesis is false?

    a. Type III

    b. Type IV

    c. Type I

    d. Type II

111. To compare the means of three or more groups simultaneously, which of the following tests is the most appropriate?

    a. Fischer's exact test

    b. Chi-squared test

    c. ANOVA

    d. Student's t-test

112. When team members express their own opinions and ideas, often disagreeing with others, this is referred to as:

    a. norming.

    b. performing.

    c. forming.

    d. storming.

113. When plotting the main effects, a greater slope of the effect indicates:

    a. confounding.

    b. aliasing.

    c. experimental error.

    d. increased interaction.

Use the following paragraph to answer questions 114–115.

ABC Manufacturing, a machine shop that uses total productive maintenance methodologies, received a purchase order from their customer for 50 parts. Because of ABC's experience with manufacturing and the long lead time to produce these parts, ABC creates a production order for 55 parts to ensure that they will complete at least 50 parts.

114. It can be assumed that they most likely reason ABC is producing 55 parts instead of 50 parts is due to what type of waste?

    a. Defects

    b. Transportation

    c. Inventory

    d. Overproduction

115. Producing 55 parts when the order was for 50 is an example of what type of waste?

    a. Inventory

    b. Defects

    c. Overproduction

    d. Processing

116. The act of conducting performance or process benchmarking within an organization by comparing similar business units or business processes is:

    a. focused benchmarking.

    b. strategic benchmarking.

    c. functional benchmarking.

    d. internal benchmarking.

117. A Six Sigma professional wants to determine with 95% confidence whether the mean fill weight differs by 1 g after making an adjustment to the process. The process historical $\sigma = 3.5$ g. What is the minimum required sample size?

    a. 90

    b. 48

    c. 53

    d. 60

118. What is the process capability on an attributes control chart?

    a.   The process average

    b.   Plus or minus half of the control limits

    c.   The same as a variables control chart

    d.   None of these

119. This tool is used in the design process to minimize or prevent failures, and improve safety and quality.

    a.   PDCA

    b.   DFSS

    c.   FMEA

    d.   SWOT

120. Calculate the x upper control limit given the following information for an $\bar{X}$ and R chart: $\bar{\bar{X}}$ 904.573, r bar 36.933, n 5.

    a.   926

    b.   987

    c.   883

    d.   904

121. The causal factor or factors that, if removed, will prevent the recurrence of the same situation describe:

    a.   root cause analysis.

    b.   FMEA.

    c.   process control.

    d.   root cause.

122. An R chart is used rather than an s chart because it is:

    a.   more accurate.

    b.   more sensitive to variations.

    c.   easier to calculate.

    d.   all of these.

123. The refill line on a bulk container is an example of:

   a. reliability-based maintenance.

   b. process capability.

   c. maintenance analytics.

   d. visual controls.

124. The scheduling of maintenance tasks based on operating conditions is referred to as condition-based maintenance. Which of the following is an example of condition-based maintenance?

   a. Spot welding tips must be dressed or changed more frequently when used on galvanized steel.

   b. Performing an oil change every 5000 miles in an automobile.

   c. A timing belt that has a high probability of failure at 70,000 miles might be scheduled for replacement at 60,000 miles.

   d. A bearing that usually fails between 1800 and 2600 hours, causing a major shutdown, might be replaced on the weekend after it has had 1500 hours of service.

125. A technique to compare the *F* value of the factor/level with an *F*-distribution value is called:

   a. full factorials.

   b. analysis of variance.

   c. fractional factorials.

   d. orthogonal design.

126. How many treatment conditions are there for seven factors, with each factor having three levels?

   a. 2187

   b. 4

   c. 10

   d. 343

127. Which of the following best describes the goal of total productive maintenance?

   a. To ensure that proper production planning has occurred prior to the issuing of material

   b. To ensure that there are no unplanned delays in production

   c. To reduce waste from the production line

   d. To perform maintenance in a timely manner

128. How many runs are necessary in a full factorial experiment with five factors, with each factor having two levels?

   a. 32

   b. 10

   c. 25

   d. 2

129. Process improvement teams should have training on which of the following topics?

   a. Project management

   b. Program management

   c. Process dynamics

   d. Team building

130. An FMEA has a severity of 7, a probability of occurrence of 5, and a probability of detection of 3. What is the RPN?

   a. 105

   b. 35

   c. 12

   d. 15

131. A visual identification of many potential causes of a problem is referred to as a:

   a. process flowchart.

   b. cause-and-effect diagram.

   c. decision tree.

   d. check sheet.

132. Trial control limits are calculated based on at least:

    a. 15 subgroups.

    b. 35 subgroups.

    c. 5 subgroups.

    d. 25 subgroups.

133. Calculate the process capability given the following information for an *np* chart: sum of *np* 55, *k* 14, *n* 200.

    a. .376

    b. 3.929

    c. 5.791

    d. 0

134. What experimental design technique would be used when an experiment may have to be conducted over several shifts?

    a. Confounding

    b. Replication

    c. Randomization

    d. Blocking

135. This perspective provides shareholders with a direct line of sight into the health and well-being of the organization.

    a. Learning and growth perspective

    b. Internal business processes perspective

    c. Customer perspective

    d. Financial perspective

136. To maintain support throughout the change life cycle, the organization must:

    a. delegate the responsibilities to a qualified consultant.

    b. divide the responsibility and authority equally between management and the workers.

    c. appoint a management representative.

    d. provide frequent communications.

137. Which of the following tools would be the most appropriate for crisis management?

    a. Contingency planning

    b. Risk analysis

    c. PEST analysis

    d. SWOT analysis

138. A user-friendly chart for the operator to use is called a _____ chart.

    a. trend

    b. cyclical

    c. moving average

    d. median

139. According to Graham and Portny (2011), the three components of any project are scope, schedule, and:

    a. resources.

    b. time.

    c. cost.

    d. quality.

140. A tool used to monitor a process to make sure that the process improvements made are continuing to produce desired results is:

    a. a control chart.

    b. gage R&R.

    c. process metrics.

    d. a control plan.

141. If an experimenter wished to have two factors at two levels, and one factor at three levels, which type of experimental design would be appropriate?

    a. Full factorial

    b. Taguchi

    c. Fractional factorial

    d. Mixture

142. Which of the following is a method of counting events?

  a. Outcomes

  b. Combination

  c. Addition

  d. Division

143. An evaluation method for a set of solutions that involves manufacturing a smaller production run of production-equivalent parts is called a:

  a. prototype.

  b. simulation.

  c. pilot run.

  d. model.

144. An evaluation method for a set of solutions that is similar to the production part in form, fit, and function, minus some features, is a:

  a. pilot run.

  b. prototype.

  c. simulation.

  d. model.

145. Forces that are for a change or decision are called:

  a. resisting forces.

  b. driving forces.

  c. advocate forces.

  d. positive forces.

Use the table below to answer questions 146–147.

	Weight value	Potential solution			
		A	B	C	D
Implementation cost	0.3	1	3	4	2
Maintenance	0.25	4	2	1	3
Reliability	0.1	4	1	2	3
Loss of customer goodwill	0.35	2.5	2.5	4	1
		2.575	2.375	3.05	2

146. Which criterion is the most important according to the ranking matrix?

    a. Loss of customer goodwill

    b. Maintenance

    c. Reliability

    d. Implementation cost

147. Which solution is the best according to the ranking matrix?

    a. C

    b. A

    c. D

    d. B

148. Forces that are against a change or decision are called:

    a. positive forces.

    b. advocate forces.

    c. driving forces.

    d. resisting forces.

149. An evaluation method for a set of solutions that uses a smaller physical representation of the production part is a:

    a. prototype.

    b. pilot run.

    c. simulation.

    d. model.

150. Those causes of variation that are large in magnitude and are not part of the normal variation are:

    a. chance causes.

    b. assignable causes.

    c. fluctuating causes.

    d. stable causes.

ANSWERS

1. b; Master Black Belt (MBB)—A Six Sigma role associated with an individual typically assigned full-time to train and mentor Black Belts as well as lead the strategy to ensure that the improvement projects chartered are the right strategic projects for the organization. Master Black Belts are usually the authorizing body to certify Green Belts and Black Belts. [I.B.1]

2. a; Mentoring/coaching is used on a one-to-one basis to teach job-specific skills. [III.D.2]

3. b; RACI model (responsible, accountable, consulted, and informed). The RACI matrix is usefully defined in detail by a team or committee, and in some cases by an individual. The roles are:

   - *Responsible.* Individuals who actively participate in an activity.

   - *Accountable.* The individual ultimately accountable for results. Only one individual may be accountable at a time.

   - *Consulted.* Individuals who must be consulted before a decision is made.

   - *Informed.* Individuals who must be informed about a decision because they are affected. These individuals do not need to take part in the decision-making process.

   [IV.C.1]

4. a; A system is a group of interdependent processes and people that together perform a common mission. [I.A.3]

5. c; Brainstorming is a group process used to generate ideas in a nonjudgmental way. The purpose of brainstorming is to generate a great deal of ideas about an issue. [III.C.3]

6. a; Skewness measures the degree to which a set of data is not symmetrical. [V.D.1]

7. d; The tree diagram is a tool that depicts the hierarchy of tasks and subtasks needed to complete an objective. The finished diagram resembles a tree. Tree diagrams may be depicted either vertically (top–down) or horizontally (left to right). When depicted top–down, tasks move from general (top) to specific (down), and when depicted left-to-right, tasks move from left (general) to right (specific). [IV.D]

8. d; Announcements (formal or informal) are communications used acknowledge a key milestone. [II.A]

9. a; The critical path is the path from start to finish that requires the most time. [IV.D]

10. b; Benchmarking provides an organization with the opportunity to see what level of process performance is possible. [II.B]

11. c; Education focuses on broadening an individual's knowledge base and expanding thinking processes. Training is considered a subset of education that focuses on increasing proficiency in a skill. [III.D.1]

12. b; According to Williams (2008), the four components of any project are scope, quality, time, and cost. [IV.B.5]

13. a; When a tolerance specification is changed, the % tolerance variation will likely have been impacted. This will require an evaluation or possible re-execution of the gage R&R study. [VIII.C.1]

14. d; Black Belt (BB)—A Six Sigma role associated with an individual typically assigned full-time to train and mentor Green Belts as well as lead improvement projects using specified methodologies such as DMAIC, DMADV (define, measure, analyze, design, verify), and DFSS. [I.B.1]

15. c; The best way to make certain that adequate provision for manufacturability and assembly has been made is to have manufacturing/assembly expertise present on the design team. Other strategies to consider:

    1. Minimize part count.

    2. Design parts so they can be used on either side.

    3. Use off-the-shelf parts, standard components, and purchased parts.

    4. Use modular design where possible.

    [IX.B]

16. d; This approach combines the individual concepts of lean and Six Sigma, and recognizes that both are necessary to effectively drive sustained improvement. [I.A.2]

17. a; Define, measure, analyze, design, validate (DMADV) is a well-recognized design for Six Sigma (DFSS) methodology. [IX.A]

18. d; If a tray holds 30 parts, of which there are six defective parts, and you sample one part from the tray, the probability that it will be a defective part is calculated by

    $$P_{tray} = 3030 = 1.0 \text{ or } 100\%$$

    $$P_{good} = 2430 = 0.08 \text{ or } 80\%$$

    $$P_{bad} = 630 = 0.02 \text{ or } 20\%$$

If one part is drawn at random, the probability that it is defective is 20%. [V.E.1]

19. b; A stakeholder is defined as anyone with an interest or rights in an issue, or anyone who can affect or be affected by an action or change. [II.A]

20. a; The nominal group technique (NGT) is used to prioritize a list of items. The technique begins with all team members writing their ideas down on a slip of paper without any discussion. [III.C.3]

21. b; Kurtosis measures the degree to which a set of data is peaked or flat. [V.D.1]

22. a; Team norming is when members begin to understand the need to operate as a team rather than as a group of individuals. [III.B.2]

23. b; SOP 115 Production Control Documentation needs to be updated. However, Todd Jones, Production Manager, is on vacation for six weeks.

    Because the production manager directly reports to the VP of operations, it would be appropriate for the VP of operations and the quality manager to approve the changes to the document. [VIII.D.2]

24. a; The auditor noticed that Production Batch Record 1234 was approved for release on 3/14/2016, scanned, and saved to the cloud-based server. The auditor asked for the original paper copy. The VP of operations informed the auditor that under the procedure scanned electronic copies are acceptable as the permanent record. This would not constitute a violation of the procedure. However, if the scan copy were not legible, it could be a violation of the procedure. [VIII.D.2]

25. a; SOP 110 Preventive Maintenance needs to be updated. However, Jane Doe, Maintenance Manager, was promoted to director of operations, and a replacement was recently hired. The procedure was originally approved 10/1/2015 by maintenance manager Jane Doe and Bill Smith, Quality Manager. The procedure should be signed by the same function, not necessarily the same individual. Therefore, the maintenance manager and the quality manager should both approve the changes to the procedure. [VIII.D.2]

26. d; In the Kano model for customer satisfaction, requirements that will cause dissatisfaction if not present but will cause very little satisfaction if they are present are known as *expected requirements*. [IV.A.3]

27. c; Benchmarking requires the use of a strict methodology. It must be planned and funded or it will likely fail. [II.B]

28. d; Cycle time is the time required to complete one unit from the beginning of the process to the end of the process. [V.A.1]

29. a; The variance is 67.79 for the sample set of data 45, 51, 46, 53, 46, 57, 51, 72, 55, 61.

This is an easy calculation using a simple scientific calculator. Ensure that the $n - 1$ option is selected because the data set is a sample. Typically, the calculator will give the standard deviation, which is then squared to obtain the variance. [V.D.3]

30. c; Virtual teams are made up of people in different locations who may never meet in person. Instead, the team may meet using teleconferencing facilities, or they may conduct all communication via e-mail. [III.A.1]

31. d; Juran developed the Juran trilogy: three managerial processes—quality planning, quality control, and quality improvement—for use in managing for quality. [I.A.1]

32. a; Functional requirements define how the product is to perform and under what conditions. [IX.C]

33. b; The number of degrees of freedom with n observations from a random sample, each of which could be classified into exactly one of K categories for a goodness-of-fit test with specified probabilities, is calculated by $(k - 1)$. [VI.B.7]

34. b; Customer loyalty is best measured by the following metrics: customer referrals, customer abandonment rates, and customer retention rates. [II.C.1]

35. d; Type I error occurs when the null hypothesis is rejected when it is true. We refer to the P(Type I error) = P(Rejecting H_0 when H_0 is true) = α. A type I error is also known as an α *error* and an *error of the first kind*. The P(Type I error) is also known as α-*value, producer's risk, level of significance*, and *significance level*. [VI.B.1]

		Nature (true condition)	
		H_0 is true	H_0 is false
Conclusion	H_0 is rejected	Type I error P(Type I) = a	**Correct decision**
	H_0 is not rejected	**Correct decision**	Type II error P(Type II) = b

36. a; There are four types of stakeholders: stakeholders can be supporting, opposing, helping, or hindering. [II.A]

37. c; Team champions do not generally attend regular team meetings. [III.A.2]

38. b; Genichi Taguchi argued that parts near the nominal dimension have more value than others that are within specification but farther away from the nominal value. Taguchi maintained that any deviation from nominal makes the product less valuable. This loss increases as the dimension gets farther from the nominal or "target" value. The resulting metrics are referred to as *loss functions*. [IX.C]

39. d; Individuals like to be recognized for their unique contributions. Some forms of recognition include the following:

- Letters of appreciation sent to individuals and placed in personnel files

- Public expressions of appreciation via meetings, newsletters, and so on

- Positive feedback and comments from management

- Inclusion in the performance appraisal

[III.B.1]

40. a; Walter A. Shewhart successfully brought together the disciplines of statistics, engineering, and economics and became known as the father of modern quality control. [I.A.1]

41. b; Groupthink occurs within a group of people with a desire for harmony when group members minimize conflict and reach a consensus by actively suppressing dissenting viewpoints. [III.C.1]

42. a; Customers provide specifications for products or services explicitly, *or* customers express requirements in value terms—the components that influence the buy decision—such as price, product quality, innovation, service quality, company image, and reputation, *or* customers may spotlight only their needs or wants, thus leaving it up to the organization to translate them into internal specifications. [IV.A.1]

43. b; The affinity diagram is a tool used to organize information and help achieve order out of the chaos that can develop in a brainstorming session. Large amounts of data, concepts, and ideas are grouped based on their natural relationship to one another. [IV.D]

44. c; Teams are generally better decision makers than individuals. [III.C.1]

45. b; The process capability ratio is calculated by the following formula:

$$C_{pk} = \text{Minimum of } \frac{\bar{X} - \text{LSL}}{3s}, \frac{\text{USL} - \bar{X}}{3s}$$

Given $\bar{\bar{X}}$ 904.573, USL 950, LSL 850, s 15.85,

$$904.573 - 8503 \times 15.85 = 1.148, 950 - 904.5733 \times 15.85 = 0.955$$

The smaller value is selected (0.955). A C_{pk} ratio of less than 1 is considered not capable. One possible remedy would be to center the process. [V.F.1]

46. c; For any data set that is normally distributed and for which the mean and the standard deviation are known or can be estimated, the probability of falling above or below any standard normal values or z-scores can be calculated using the following formula:

$$z = \frac{x - \mu}{\sigma}$$

For a process with a mean of 53.7 and sigma of 8.23, the percentage of product generated greater than 60 will be

$$z = \frac{60 - 53.7}{8.23} = 0.765$$

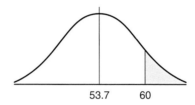

53.7   60

Look up z-value 0.765 in Appendix B Normal Distribution Probability Points—Area above Z from Durivage (2014), which yields approximately 22% of product produced will be greater than 60. [V.E.2]

47. a; Champion—A Six Sigma role associated with a senior manager who ensures that his or her projects are aligned with the organization's strategic goals and priorities, provides the Six Sigma team with resources, removes organizational barriers for the team, participates in project tollgate reviews, and essentially serves as the team's backer. A champion is also known as a *sponsor*. [I.B.2]

48. d; Competency-based training is training that is based on measurable outcomes (proficiencies). [III.D.3]

49. a; A training needs analysis is a diagnostic method for identifying the gap between current performance and desired performance. Organizational training needs stem from the strategic planning process, while individual training needs stem from both strategic planning and individual performance. [III.D.1]

50. b; Reproducibility is the precision under conditions where independent measurement results are obtained with the same method on identical measurement items with different operators using different equipment. [V.C.1]

51. a; The QFD matrix helps illustrate the linkage between the VOC and the resulting technical requirements. [IV.A.3]

52. d; The takt time to produce 1000 quarters due in five days with one eight-hour shift per day is calculated by

$$\text{Takt time} = \frac{\text{Time available}}{\text{Number of units to be produced}}$$

$$= \frac{8 \times 60 \times 5}{1000} = 2.4 \text{ minutes per unit}$$

[VII.B.2]

53. d; Under the theory of constraints, the process that receives attention is the slowest process in the system. Currently, the pressing process is the slowest. When the pressing process becomes faster than the punching process, then the punching becomes the focus. [VII.B.4]

54. a; The theory of constraints (TOC) is a problem-solving methodology that focuses on the weakest link in a chain of processes. Usually, the constraint is the slowest process. Flow rate through the system cannot increase unless the rate at the constraint increases. [VII.B.4]

55. a; Poka-yoke is a term that means to mistake-proof a process by building safeguards into the system that help avoid or immediately find errors. A poka-yoke device is one that prevents incorrect parts from being made, assembled, or stored, or that easily identifies a flaw or error. [VII.B.1]

56. d; Continuous flow manufacturing, commonly referred to as CFM, is a method in which items are produced and moved from one processing step to the next one piece at a time. Each process makes only the one piece that the next process needs, and the transfer batch size is one. CFM is sometimes known as *one-piece flow* or *single-piece flow*. [VII.B.2]

57. b; *Kaizen* is a Japanese term that means gradual, unending improvement by doing little things better and setting and achieving increasingly higher standards. [VII.B.3]

58. c; The concept behind critical to X (CtX), where X is a variable, is simply that X is an area or areas of impact on the customer. [IV.A.3]

59. d; Define, measure, analyze, improve, control (DMAIC) and define, measure, explore, develop, implement (DMEDI) methodologies both utilize a *define* phase. [IX.A]

60. a; Nominal scales classify data into categories with no order implied. [V.B.2]

61. c; This is the definition of project performance measurements. Project performance measurements help to manage the project by indicating the relative success of the project. [IV.B.5]

62. b; Takt time is the rate in time per unit at which the process must complete units in order to achieve the customer demand. [V.A.1]

63. d;

$$PTR = \frac{6\hat{\sigma}_{ms}}{USL - LSL}$$

[V.C.1]

64. d; RACI model (responsible, accountable, consulted, informed). The RACI matrix is usefully defined in detail by a team or committee, and in some cases, by an individual. The roles are:

- *Responsible.* Individuals who actively participate in an activity.

- *Accountable.* The individual ultimately accountable for results. Only one individual may be accountable at a time.

- *Consulted.* Individuals who must be consulted before a decision is made.

- *Informed.* Individuals who must be informed about a decision because they are affected. These individuals do not need to take part in the decision-making process.

[IV.C.1]

65. c; Green Belt (GB)—A Six Sigma role associated with an individual who retains his or her regular position within the firm but is trained in the tools, methods, and skills necessary to conduct Six Sigma improvement projects either individually or as part of larger teams. [I.B.1]

66. d; Gantt charts use the outputs of a work breakdown structure to map out a project timeline. [IV.C.1]

67. c; Tollgate reviews ensure that all the tasks before the review are complete, and serve as a method of organization for a project. [IV.C.1]

68. c;

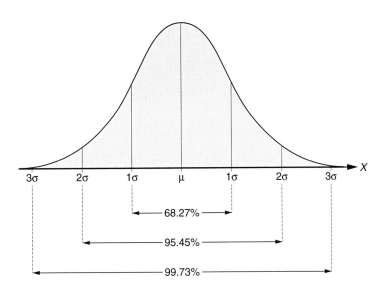

The percentages for ±1, 2 , and 3 standard deviations are provided in the figure. [V.D.1]

69. b; A key benefit of the SIPOC is that it is much easier to complete than either a process map or a value stream map. SIPOCs can be used as a basis for constructing detailed process maps and value stream maps at future dates. Furthermore, SIPOCs help identify the voice of the customer as well as provide quick oversight into the initial X's and Y's. [IV.A.3]

70. c; Tree diagrams may be used in a wide variety of situations, including critical-to-quality tree, decision tree, fault tree analysis, Gozinto chart, organization chart, process decision program chart, five whys, work breakdown structure (WBS), and so on. [IV.D]

71. b; Define, measure, analyze, design, validate (DMADV), define, measure, analyze, design, optimize, validate (DMADOV), define, measure, explore, develop, implement (DMEDI), and identify, design, optimize, validate (IDOV) design methodologies do not include a *control* phase as contained in DMAIC. The control phase is used to monitor the outputs of products and services. [IX.A]

72. a;

$$\text{Takt time} = \frac{\text{Time available}}{\text{Number of units to be produced}}$$

$$= \frac{8 \times 60}{116} = 4.14 \text{ minutes per unit}$$

[V.A.1]

73. b; A Gantt chart is a type of bar chart used in process/project planning and control to display planned work and finished work in relation to time. It is also called a *milestone chart*. The Gantt chart provides an excellent visualization of time-based progress. [IV.C.1]

74. c;

$$GRR = \sqrt{EV^2 + AV^2} = \sqrt{0.132^2 + 10.38^2} = 10.38\%$$

[V.C.1]

75. a; The project scope ensures that resources are efficiently directed at solving a problem by placing clear constraints on the project. Making the scope too broad is in direct opposition to the essence of the project scope and thus will always put the project or other projects in danger of failing. [IV.B.3]

76. d; The project scope ensures that the resources are efficiently directed at solving a problem by placing clear constraints on the project. [IV.B.3]

77. b; Team performing is when team members work together to reach their common goal. [III.B.2]

78. d; Ratio scales have meaningful differences, and an absolute zero exists. [V.B.2]

79. a; Suppliers–inputs–process–outputs–customers (SIPOC) can be used to identify stakeholders. [I.B.2]

80. b; Work in progress (WIP) is the material that has been input into the process but that has not reached the output or finished stage. This includes material being processed, waiting to be processed, or stored as inventory at each step. [V.A.1]

81. c; Team forming is when members struggle to understand the team goal and its meaning for them individually. [III.B.2]

82. b; Although the test result is recorded as pass/fail, the measurement itself is on a continuous scale. [V.B.3]

83. c; The prioritization matrix is a tool used to choose between several options that have many useful benefits, but that may not all be of equal value. The choices are prioritized according to known weighted criteria and then narrowed down to the most desirable or effective one(s) to accomplish the task or problem at hand. [IV.D]

84. d; Use the following formula to calculate the standard error for the following sample set of data: 43, 45, 40, 39, 42, 44, 41.

$$s_{\bar{X}} = \frac{s}{\sqrt{n}} = 4.67n = 1.77$$

Note: The standard deviation is 4.67 and the sample size is 7. [V.D.3]

85. c; Consensus creates a situation or outcome that all the participants can live with. If no such situation or outcome can be found, discussion continues. [III.C.3]

86. a; Good team members are characterized by actively participating in team meetings, communicating ideas and expertise, openly listening, and completing action assignments as scheduled. [III.A.3]

87. c; Appraisal costs are costs associated with the inspection and appraisal processes. [II.C.2]

88. c; A process that has an average tensile strength of 1200 psi (nominal is best) and a sample standard deviation of 160 psi derived from six samples. The signal to noise S/N_N ratio for nominal is best is calculated by

$$S/N_N = 10 \log10[(y^2/s^2) - (1/n)]$$

where

y = Process average

s = Standard deviation

n = Sample size

$S/N_N = 10 \log10[(y^2/s^2) - (1/n)] = 10 \log10[(12{,}002/1602) - (1/6)] = 17.5dB$

[IX.C]

89. b; An improvement process in which a company measures its performance against that of best-in-class companies, determines how those companies achieved their performance levels, and uses the information to improve its own performance. The subjects that can be benchmarked include strategies, operations, processes, and procedures. [I.A.2]

90. a; Whenever "or" is verbalized, the mathematical operation is addition. Refer to probability theorems 3 and 4:

Theorem 3. If A and B are two mutually exclusive events (the occurrence of one event makes the other event impossible), then the probability that either event A or event B will occur is the sum of their respective probabilities: P(A or B) = P(A) + P(B).

Theorem 4. If event A and event B are not mutually exclusive, then the probability of either event A or event B or both is given by P(A or B or both) = P(A) + P(B) − P(both).

[V.E.1]

91. d; The coefficient of determination is the correlation coefficient squared:

$$r^2 = 0.710$$

[VI.A.1]

92. b; The correlation coefficient is calculated using the following formula:

$$r = \frac{n \times \Sigma XY - \Sigma X \times \Sigma Y}{\sqrt{n \times \Sigma X^2 - (\Sigma x)^2} \times \sqrt{n \times \Sigma Y^2 - (\Sigma Y)^2}}$$

where

r = Correlation coefficient

X = The independent variable

Y = The dependent variable

n = The number of sample pairs

Time	Strength				
X	Y	XY	X^2	Y^2	
1.0	41	41	1.0	1681	
1.5	41	61.5	2.3	1681	
2.0	41	82	4.0	1681	
2.5	43	107.5	6.3	1849	
3.0	43	129	9.0	1849	
3.5	44	154	12.3	1936	
4.0	50	200	16.0	2500	
17.5	**303.0**	**775.0**	**50.8**	**13177.0**	Sum

$$r = \frac{7 \times 775 - 17.5 \times 303}{\sqrt{7 \times 50.8 - (17.5)^2} \times \sqrt{7 \times 13177 - (303)^2}} = 0.843$$

[VI.A.1]

93. a; A Pareto chart can be used to help a process improvement team focus their efforts based on the PFMEA. [VI.C]

94. b; In five years, $5000 will be available. The net present value of that money, assuming an annual interest rate of 10%, can be calculated by

$$P = F(1 + i)^{-n}$$

where

   P = Net present value

   F = Amount to be received n years from now

   i = Annual interest rate expressed as a decimal

$$\$3104.61 = \$5000(1 + 0.10)^{-5}$$

[II.C.2]

95. d; The most desirable relationship between the specification and the process spread is when $6\sigma <$ USL − LSL, as demonstrated in the figure below.

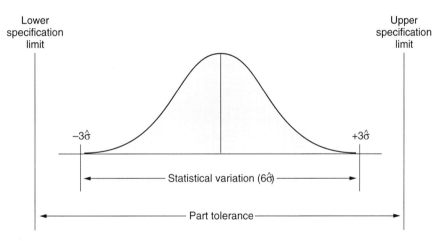

Relationship between statistical control limits and product specifications.

Source: Adapted from Durivage (2014). Used with permission.

[V.F.1]

96. b; To calculate the 95% confidence interval for the average if the sample size is 75, the mean of a sample drawn from a population is 2.15, and the population standard deviation is known to be 0.8, use

$$\bar{X} \pm Z_{\alpha/2} \frac{\sigma}{\sqrt{n}}$$

where

X = The point estimate of the average

σ = The population standard deviation

n = The sample size

$Z_{\alpha/2}$ = The normal distribution value for a given confidence level (see Appendix D, Selected Double-Sided Normal Distribution Probability Points from Durivage (2014).

$$\bar{X} \pm Z_{\alpha/2} \frac{\sigma}{\sqrt{n}} = 2.15 \pm 1.960 \times \frac{0.8}{\sqrt{75}} = 2.15 \pm 0.181 = 1.969 \text{ to } 2.331$$

The 95% confidence interval is 1.969 to 2.331. [VI.B.4]

97. d; For a process with a mean of 53.7 and sigma of 8.23, the value (x) for the lower specification limit that will yield 5% scrap can be calculated by

$$x = \mu - z\sigma$$

Look up z-value 1.665 (note that the minus sign can be dropped) in Appendix B, Normal Distribution Probability Points—Area above Z from Durivage (2014). The z-value is approximately 1.65.

$$x = 53.7 - 1.65 \times 8.23 = 40$$

A lower value of 40 will yield approximately 5% scrap. [V.E.2]

98. c; The numerator of the capability index equation is the tolerance.

$$C_p = \frac{USL - LSL}{6s} > 1$$

[V.F.1]

99. d; This figure demonstrates positive correlation. The points fall on a straight line increasing from left to right. However, the correlation is not perfect due to the width (dispersion) of the points.

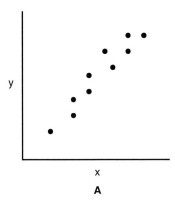

A

[VI.A.1]

100. c; This figure demonstrates nearly perfect negative correlation. The points fall on a straight line decreasing from left to right.

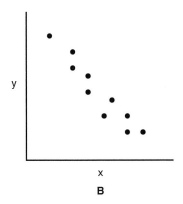

B

[VI.A.1]

101. c; Interaction is when two or more factors, together, produce a result different than their separate effects. [VII.A.2]

102. d; To calculate the process capability for an *np* chart, the centerline must first be calculated using the following formula:

$$\overline{np} = \frac{\Sigma np}{k} \text{ (Centerline)}$$

where

    n = Subgroup size

    np = (Subgroup count)

    k = The number of subgroups

Given the sum of np 55, k 14,

$$np = \frac{55}{14} = 3.929$$

For attributes control charts, the process capability is simply the centerline of the control chart, in this case, 3.929. [V.F.4]

103. c; Detection is the likelihood that current controls will prevent a failure from reaching the customer. [VI.C]

104. a; A kanban is a system that signals the need to replenish stock or materials or to produce more of an item. Kanban is also known as a "pull" approach. [VII.B.1]

105. a; The control plan should specify a sampling plan that experience has shown to be effective in detecting changes to the process. The plan should identify gages or fixtures to be used. If measurements are to be made, the plan should cross-reference a control plan for monitoring GR&R for the gage involved. [VIII.C.2]

106. c; Number 1 represents a primary event.

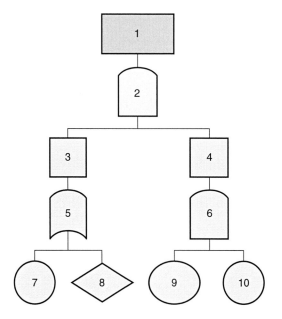

[VI.D.2]

107. b; Numbers 2 and 6 represent AND gates.

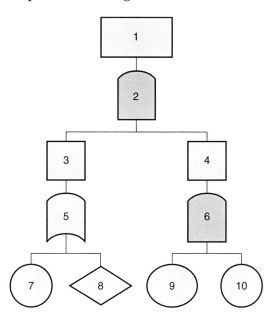

[VI.D.2]

108. d; Number 5 represents an OR gate.

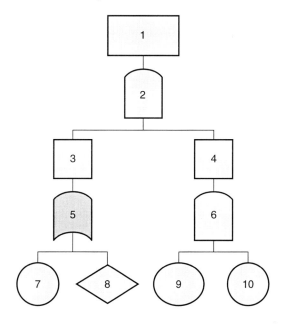

[VI.D.2]

109. a; When constructing a Pareto diagram, the "other" category is placed in the last column. Because there are many types of minor defects that are few in quantity, they are collected in this category. There is no real need to identify them by specific type since they make up the "trivial many" and will not be investigated. [VI.D.2]

110. d; Type II error occurs when the alternative hypothesis is not rejected when it is false. We refer to the P(Type II error) = P(Not rejecting H_0 when H_0 is false) = β. A type II error is also known as a β *error* and an *error of the second kind.*

		Nature (true condition)	
		H_0 is true	H_0 is false
Conclusion	H_0 is rejected	Type I error P(Type I) = a	**Correct decision**
	H_0 is not rejected	**Correct decision**	Type II error P(Type II) = b

[V1.B.1]

111. c; To compare the means of three or more groups simultaneously, an ANOVA is the most appropriate test. In its simplest form, ANOVA provides a statistical test of whether or not the means of three or more groups are equal, and therefore generalizes the *t*-test to more than two groups. Doing multiple two-sample *t*-tests would result in an increased chance of committing a type I error. For this reason, ANOVAs are useful in comparing three or more means for statistical significance. [VI.B.6]

112. d; Team storming is when members express their own opinions and ideas, often disagreeing with others. [III.B.2]

113. d; Type II error occurs when the alternative hypothesis is not rejected when it is false. We refer to the P(Type II error) = P(Not rejecting H_0 when H_0 is false) = β. A type II error is also known as a β *error* and an *error of the second kind.*

		Nature (true condition)	
		H_0 is true	H_0 is false
Conclusion	H_0 is rejected	Type I error P(Type I) = a	**Correct decision**
	H_0 is not rejected	**Correct decision**	Type II error P(Type II) = b

[VI.B.1]

114. a; ABC is producing 55 parts instead of 50 parts due to defects. The overproduction of parts is considered to be a form of waste. [VI.D.3]

115. c; ABC producing 55 parts when the order is for 50 is an example of overproduction. Overproduction is considered to be a form of waste. [VI.D.3]

116. d; Internal benchmarking is the act of conducting performance or process benchmarking within an organization by comparing similar business units or business processes. [II.B]

117. b; To calculate the minimum sample size required with 95% confidence if the mean fill weight differs by 1 g after making an adjustment to the process (historical σ = 3.5 g), use the following formula:

$$n = \left(\frac{z_{\alpha/2}\sigma}{E} \right)^2$$

where

σ = Standard deviation

E = Difference to detect

$z_{\alpha/2}$ = The normal distribution value for a given confidence level

$n = (1.96 \times 3.51)^2 = 47.06$, rounded up 48

Forty-eight samples are needed to detect a difference of 1 g for a process with a historical standard deviation of 3.5.

See Appendix D, Selected Single-Sided Normal Distribution Probability Points Factors from Durivage (2014). [VI.B.3]

118. a; The process capability on an attributes control chart is simply the centerline of the attributes control chart (process average). [V.F.4]

119. c; FMEA is used in the design process to minimize or prevent failures, and improve safety and quality. [VI.C]

120. a; To calculate the x upper control limit for an $\bar{X}$ and R chart given $\bar{\bar{X}}$ 904.573, $\bar{R}$ 36.933, n 5, use the following formula:

$$\bar{X}\ \text{UCL} = \bar{\bar{X}} + A_2 \times \bar{R}_K$$

$$X\ \text{UCL} = 904.573 + 0.577 \times 36.933 = 926$$

For A_2, see Appendix O, Control Chart Constants, from Durivage (2014). [VIII.A.5]

121. d; Solving a process problem means identifying the root cause and eliminating it. The ultimate test of whether the root cause has been eliminated is the ability to toggle the problem on and off by removing and reintroducing the root cause. [VI.D.2]

122. c; An R chart is used rather than an s chart because it is easier to calculate. An R chart is just a simple subtraction of the low value from the high vale in a subgroup, whereas an s chart requires the calculation of the subgroup's standard deviation. [VIII.A.4]

123. d; Visual controls are approaches and techniques that permit one to visually determine the status of a system, factory, or process at a glance, and prevent or minimize process variation. To some degree, it can be viewed as a minor form of mistake-proofing. [VIII.B.2]

124. a; Condition-based maintenance is the scheduling of maintenance tasks based on operating conditions. Spot welding tips that must be dressed or changed more frequently when used on galvanized steel is an example of condition-based maintenance. [VIII.B.1]

125. b; An ANOVA technique is used to compare the F value of the factor/level with an F-distribution value. [VII.A.4]

126. a; The number of runs required for a full factorial experiment with seven factors, with each factor having three levels, is calculated by

$$n = L^F$$

where

    n = Number of runs

    L = Number of levels

    F = Number of factors

$$n = 3^7 = 2187$$

[VII.A.1]

127. b; Total productive maintenance (TPM) is a methodology that works to ensure that every machine in a production process is always able to perform its required tasks so that production is never interrupted. TPM maximizes equipment effectiveness by using a preventive maintenance program throughout the life of the equipment. [VIII.B.1]

128. a; The number of runs required for a full factorial experiment with five factors, with each factor having two levels, is calculated by

$$n = L^F$$

where

    n = Number of runs

    L = Number of levels

    F = Number of factors

$$n = 2^5 = 32$$

[VII.A.1]

129. d; Without an understanding of how a team works and the individual behavior that advances team progress, the team will often get caught in personality concerns and turf wars. [III.A.4]

130. a; To calculate the RPN for an FMEA with a severity of 7, a probability of occurrence of 5, and a probability of detection of 3, the following formula is used:

$$RPN = S \times O \times D = 7 \times 5 \times 3 = 105$$

where

S = Severity

O = Probability of occurrence

D = Probability of detection

[VI.C]

131. b; A cause-and-effect diagram (also called the *Ishikawa diagram* or *fishbone diagram*) traditionally divides causes into several generic categories. In use, a large empty diagram is often drawn on a whiteboard or flip chart to visually display potential causes of a problem. [VI.D.2]

132. d; Trial control limits are calculated based on at least 25 subgroups. [VIII.A.4]

133. b; The process capability for an *np* chart is simply the process average. Given the following information—sum of *np* 55, *k* 14, *n* 200—the calculation is

$$\overline{np} = \frac{\Sigma np}{k} \ (\text{Centerline}) = \frac{55}{14} = 3.929$$

[VIII.A.4]

134. d; Randomization is used to assign treatments to experimental units so that each unit has an equal chance of being assigned a particular treatment, thus minimizing the effect of variation from uncontrolled noise factors. [VII.A.2]

135. d; The financial perspective provides shareholders with a direct line of sight into the health and well-being of the organization. [II.C.1]

136. b; Continuous communication of the status throughout the change cycle is the key to maintaining support. [I.B.2]

137. a; Contingency planning (also called a *plan B*) is used for crisis management, business continuity, and asset security. [I.A.4]

138. d; A median chart is user-friendly for the operator as the middle value is used and the calculation of the subgroup average is not required. [VIII.A.4]

139. a; According to Graham and Portny (2011), the three components of any project are scope, schedule, and resources. [IV.B.5]

140. a; Once a process has been improved, it must be monitored to ensure that the gains are maintained and to determine when additional improvements are required. Control charts are used to monitor the stability of the process and determine when a special cause is present, and when to take appropriate action. [VIII.D.4]

141. b; If an experimenter wished to have two factors at one level and one factor at three levels, a Taguchi design would be the most appropriate choice. There are also some Taguchi designs that combine two-level and three-level factors. [VII.A.3]

142. b; A combination is a counting technique that requires the unordered arrangement of a set of objects.

$$C(n,k) = \frac{n!}{(n-k)!k!}$$

where C is the number of ways to combine k items from a set of n. [V.E.1]

143. c; An evaluation method for a set of solutions that involves manufacturing a smaller production run of production-equivalent parts is a pilot run. [VII.C]

144. b; An evaluation method for a set of solutions that is similar to the production part in form, fit, and function, minus some features, is a prototype. [VII.C]

145. b; Forces that are for a change or decision are called *driving forces*. [VII.C]

146. a;

Specific criteria	Weight value	Potential solution			
		A	B	C	D
Implementation cost	0.3	1	3	4	2
Maintenance	0.25	4	2	1	3
Reliability	0.1	4	1	2	3
Loss of customer goodwill	0.35	2.5	2.5	4	1
		2.575	2.375	3.05	2

Loss of customer goodwill has the highest associated weight value. [VII.C]

147. a;

		Potential solution			
Specific criteria	Weight value	A	B	C	D
Implementation cost	0.3	1	3	4	2
Maintenance	0.25	4	2	1	3
Reliability	0.1	4	1	2	3
Loss of customer goodwill	0.35	2.5	2.5	4	1
		2.575	2.375	3.05	2

Solution C is the best solution as it has the highest total weighted value. [VII.C]

148. d; Forces that are against a change or decision are called *resisting forces*. [VII.C]

149. d; An evaluation method for a set of solutions that uses a smaller physical representation of the production part is a model. [VII.C]

150. b; Those causes of variation that are large in magnitude and are not part of the normal variation are assignable or special causes. [VIII.A.5]

Appendix
Certified Six Sigma Black Belt (CSSBB) Body of Knowledge

The topics in this Body of Knowledge include additional detail in the form of subtext explanations and the cognitive level at which test questions will be written. This information will provide guidance for the candidate preparing to take the exam. The subtext is not intended to limit the subject matter or be all-inclusive of what might be covered in an exam. It is meant to clarify the type of content to be included in the exam. The descriptor in parentheses at the end of each entry refers to the maximum cognitive level at which the topic will be tested. A complete description of cognitive levels is provided at the end of this document.

I. Organization-wide Planning and Deployment (12 Questions)

A. *Organization-wide considerations*

1. *Fundamentals of six sigma and lean methodologies.* Define and describe the value, foundations, philosophy, history, and goals of these approaches, and describe the integration and complementary relationship between them. (Understand)

2. *Six sigma, lean, and continuous improvement methodologies.* Describe when to use six sigma instead of other problem-solving approaches, and describe the importance of aligning six sigma objectives with organizational goals. Describe screening criteria and how such criteria can be used for the selection of six sigma projects, lean initiatives, and other continuous improvement methods. (Apply)

3. *Relationships among business systems and processes.* Describe the interactive relationships among business systems, processes, and internal and external stakeholders , and the impact those relationships have on business systems. (Understand)

4. *Strategic planning and deployment for initiatives.* Define the importance of strategic planning for six sigma projects and lean initiatives. Demonstrate how hoshin kanri (X-matrix), portfolio analysis, and other tools can be used in support of strategic deployment of these projects. Use feasibility

studies, SWOT analysis (strengths, weaknesses, opportunities, and threats), PEST analysis (political, economic, social, and technological) and contingency planning and business continuity planning to enhance strategic planning and deployment. (Apply)

B. *Leadership*

1. *Roles and responsibilities.* Describe the roles and responsibilities of executive leadership, champions, sponsors, process owners, master black belts, black belts, and green belts in driving six sigma and lean initiatives. Describe how each group influences project deployment in terms of providing or managing resources, enabling changes in organizational structure, and supporting communications about the purpose and deployment of the initiatives. (Understand)

2. *Organizational roadblocks and change management.* Describe how an organization's structure and culture can impact six sigma projects. Identify common causes of six sigma failures, including lack of management support and lack of resources. Apply change management techniques, including stakeholder analysis, readiness assessments, and communication plans to overcome barriers and drive organization-wide change. (Apply)

II. Organizational Process Management and Measures (10 Questions)

A. *Impact on stakeholders.* Describe the impact six sigma projects can have on customers, suppliers, and other stakeholders. (Understand)

B. *Benchmarking.* Define and distinguish between various types of benchmarking, e.g., best practices, competitive, collaborative, breakthrough. Select measures and performance goals for projects resulting from benchmarking activities. (Apply)

C. *Business measures*

1. *Performance measures.* Define and describe balanced scorecard, key performance indicators (KPIs), customer loyalty metrics, and leading and lagging indicators. Explain how to create a line of sight from performance measures to organizational strategies. (Analyze)

2. *Financial measures.* Define and use revenue growth, market share, margin, net present value (NPV), return on investment (ROI), and cost–benefit analysis (CBA). Explain the difference between hard cost measures (from profit and loss statements) and soft cost benefits of cost avoidance and reduction. (Apply)

III. Team Management (18 Questions)

A. *Team formation*

1. *Team types and constraints.* Define and describe various teams, including virtual, cross-functional, and self-directed. Determine what team type will work best for a given set of constraints, e.g., geography, technology availability, staff schedules, time zones. (Apply)

2. *Team roles and responsibilities.* Define and describe various team roles and responsibilities for leader, facilitator, coach, and individual member. (Understand)

3. *Team member selection criteria.* Describe various factors that influence the selection of team members, including the ability to influence, openness to change, required skills sets, subject matter expertise, and availability. (Apply)

4. *Team success factors.* Identify and describe the elements necessary for successful teams, e.g., management support, clear goals, ground rules, timelines. (Apply)

B. *Team facilitation*

1. *Motivational techniques.* Describe and apply techniques to motivate team members. Identify factors that can demotivate team members and describe techniques to overcome them. (Apply)

2. *Team stages of development.* Identify and describe the classic stages of team development: forming, storming, norming, performing, and adjourning. (Apply)

3. *Team communication.* Describe and explain the elements of an effective communication plan, e.g., audience identification, message type, medium, frequency. (Apply)

4. *Team leadership models.* Describe and select appropriate leadership approaches (e.g., direct, coach, support, delegate) to ensure team success. (Apply)

C. *Team dynamics*

1. *Group behaviors.* Identify and use various conflict resolution techniques (e.g., coaching, mentoring, intervention) to overcome negative group dynamics, including dominant and reluctant participants, groupthink, rushing to finish, and digressions. (Evaluate)

2. *Meeting management.* Select and use various meeting management techniques, including using agendas, starting on time, requiring pre-work by attendees, and ensuring that the right people and resources are available. (Apply)

3. *Team decision-making methods.* Define, select, and use various tools (e.g., consensus, nominal group technique, multi-voting) for decision-making. (Apply)

D. *Team training*

1. *Needs assessment.* Identify the steps involved to implement an effective training curriculum: identify skills gaps, develop learning objectives, prepare a training plan, and develop training materials. (Understand)

2. *Delivery.* Describe various techniques used to deliver effective training, including adult learning theory, soft skills, and modes of learning. (Understand)

3. *Evaluation.* Describe various techniques to evaluate training, including evaluation planning, feedback surveys, pre-training and post-training testing. (Understand)

IV. Define (20 questions)

A. *Voice of the customer*

1. *Customer identification.* Identify and segment customers and show how a project will impact both internal and external customers. (Apply)

2. *Customer data collection.* Identify and select appropriate data collection methods (e.g., surveys, focus groups, interviews, observations) to gather voice of the customer data. Ensure the data collection methods used are reviewed for validity and reliability. (Analyze)

3. *Customer requirements.* Define, select, and apply appropriate tools to determine customer needs and requirements, including critical-to-X (CTX when 'X' can be quality, cost, safety, etc.), CTQ tree, quality function deployment (QFD), supplier, input, process, output, customer (SIPOC) and Kano model. (Analyze)

B. *Business case and project charter*

1. *Business case.* Describe business case justification used to support projects. (Understand)

2. *Problem statement.* Develop a project problem statement and evaluate it in relation to baseline performance and improvement goals. (Evaluate)

3. *Project scope.* Develop and review project boundaries to ensure that the project has value to the customer. (Analyze)

4. *Goals and objectives.* Identify SMART (specific, measureable, actionable, relevant and time bound) goals and objectives on the basis of the project's problem statement and scope. (Analyze)

5. *Project performance measurements.* Identify and evaluate performance measurements (e.g., cost, revenue, delivery, schedule, customer satisfaction) that connect critical elements of the process to key outputs. (Analyze)

6. *Project charter review.* Explain the importance of having periodic project charter reviews with stakeholders. (Understand)

C. *Project management (PM) tools.* Identify and use the following PM tools to track projects and document their progress. (Evaluate)

1. *Gantt charts*

2. *Toll-gate reviews*

3. *Work breakdown structure (WBS)*

4. *RACI model (responsible, accountable, consulted and informed)*

D. *Analytical tools.* Identify and use the following analytical tools throughout the DMAIC cycle. (Apply)

1. *Affinity diagrams*

2. *Tree diagrams*

3. *Matrix diagrams*

4. *Prioritization matrices*

5. *Activity network diagrams*

V. Measure (25 Questions)

A. *Process characteristics*

1. *Process flow metrics.* Identify and use process flow metrics (e.g., work in progress [WIP], work in queue [WIQ], touch time, takt time, cycle time, throughput) to determine constraints. Describe the impact that "hidden factories" can have on process flow metrics. (Analyze)

2. *Process analysis tools.* Select, use and evaluate various tools, e.g., value stream maps, process maps, work instructions, flowcharts, spaghetti diagrams, circle diagrams, gemba walk. (Evaluate)

B. *Data collection*

1. *Types of data.* Define, classify, and distinguish between qualitative and quantitative data, and continuous and discrete data. (Evaluate)

2. *Measurement scales.* Define and use nominal, ordinal, interval, and ratio measurement scales. (Apply)

3. *Sampling.* Define and describe sampling concepts, including representative selection, homogeneity, bias, accuracy, and precision. Determine the appropriate sampling method (e.g., random, stratified, systematic, subgroup, block) to obtain valid representation in various situations. (Evaluate)

4. *Data collection plans and methods.* Develop and implement data collection plans that include data capture and processing tools, e.g., check sheets, data coding, data cleaning (imputation techniques). Avoid data collection pitfalls by defining the metrics to be used or collected, ensuring that collectors are trained in the tools and understand how the data will be used, and checking for seasonality effects. (Analyze)

C. *Measurement systems*

1. *Measurement system analysis (MSA).* Use gauge repeatability and reproducibility (R&R) studies and other MSA tools (e.g., bias, correlation, linearity, precision to tolerance, percent agreement) to analyze measurement system capability. (Evaluate)

2. *Measurement systems across the organization.* Identify how measurement systems can be applied to marketing, sales, engineering, research and development (R&D), supply chain management, and customer satisfaction data. (Understand)

3. *Metrology.* Define and describe elements of metrology, including calibration systems, traceability to reference standards, and the control and integrity of measurement devices and standards. (Understand)

D. *Basic statistics*

1. *Basic statistical terms.* Define and distinguish between population parameters and sample statistics, e.g., proportion, mean, standard deviation. (Apply)

2. *Central limit theorem.* Explain the central limit theorem and its significance in the application of inferential statistics for confidence intervals, hypothesis tests, and control charts. (Understand)

3. *Descriptive statistics.* Calculate and interpret measures of dispersion and central tendency. (Evaluate)

4. *Graphical methods.* Construct and interpret diagrams and charts, e.g., box-and-whisker plots, scatter diagrams, histograms, normal probability plots, frequency distributions, cumulative frequency distributions. (Evaluate)

5. *Valid statistical conclusions.* Distinguish between descriptive and inferential statistical studies. Evaluate how the results of statistical studies are used to draw valid conclusions. (Evaluate)

E. Probability

1. *Basic concepts.* Describe and apply probability concepts, e.g., independence, mutually exclusive events, addition and multiplication rules, conditional probability, complementary probability, joint occurrence of events. (Apply)

2. *Distributions.* Describe, interpret, and use various distributions, e.g., normal, Poisson, binomial, chi square, Student's t, F, hypergeometric, bivariate, exponential, lognormal, Weibull. (Evaluate)

F. *Process capability*

1. *Process capability indices.* Define, select, and calculate C_p and C_{pk}. (Evaluate)

2. *Process performance indices.* Define, select, and calculate P_p, P_{pk}, C_{pm}, and process sigma. (Evaluate)

3. *General process capability studies.* Describe and apply elements of designing and conducting process capability studies relative to characteristics, specifications, sampling plans, stability and normality. (Evaluate)

4. *Process capability for attributes data.* Calculate the process capability and process sigma level for attributes data. (Apply)

5. *Process capability for non-normal data.* Identify non-normal data and determine when it is appropriate to use Box-Cox or other transformation techniques. (Apply)

6. *Process performance vs. specification.* Distinguish between natural process limits and specification limits. Calculate process performance metrics, e.g., percent defective, parts per million (PPM), defects per million opportunities (DPMO), defects per unit (DPU), throughput yield, rolled throughput yield (RTY). (Evaluate)

7. *Short-term and long-term capability.* Describe and use appropriate assumptions and conventions when only short-term data or only long-term data are available. Interpret the relationship between short-term and long-term capability. (Evaluate)

VI. Analyze (22 Questions)

A. *Measuring and modeling relationships between variables*

1. *Correlation coefficient.* Calculate and interpret the correlation coefficient and its confidence interval, and describe the difference between correlation and causation. (Evaluate)

2. *Linear regression.* Calculate and interpret regression analysis, and apply and interpret hypothesis tests for regression statistics. Use the regression model for estimation and prediction, analyze the uncertainty in the estimate, and perform a residuals analysis to validate the model. (Evaluate)

3. *Multivariate tools.* Use and interpret multivariate tools (e.g., factor analysis, discriminant analysis, multiple analysis of variance [MANOVA]) to investigate sources of variation. (Evaluate)

B. *Hypothesis testing*

1. *Terminology.* Define and interpret the significance level, power, type I, and type II errors of statistical tests. (Evaluate)

2. *Statistical vs. practical significance.* Define, compare, and interpret statistical and practical significance. (Evaluate)

3. *Sample size.* Calculate sample size for common hypothesis tests: equality of means and equality of proportions. (Apply)

4. *Point and interval estimates.* Define and distinguish between confidence and prediction intervals. Define and interpret the efficiency and bias of estimators. Calculate tolerance and confidence intervals. (Evaluate)

5. *Tests for means, variances, and proportions.* Use and interpret the results of hypothesis tests for means, variances, and proportions. (Evaluate)

6. *Analysis of variance (ANOVA).* Select, calculate, and interpret the results of ANOVAs. (Evaluate)

7. *Goodness-of-fit (chi square) tests.* Define, select, and interpret the results of these tests. (Evaluate)

8. *Contingency tables.* Select, develop, and use contingency tables to determine statistical significance. (Evaluate)

9. *Non-parametric tests.* Understand the importance of the Kruskal-Wallis and Mann-Whitney tests and when they should be used. (Understand)

C. *Failure mode and effects analysis (FMEA).* Describe the purpose and elements of FMEA, including risk priority number (RPN), and evaluate FMEA results for processes, products, and services. Distinguish between design FMEA (DFMEA) and process FMEA (PFMEA), and interpret their results. (Evaluate)

D. *Additional analysis methods*

1. *Gap analysis.* Analyze scenarios to identify performance gaps, and compare current and future states using predefined metrics. (Analyze)

2. *Root cause analysis.* Define and describe the purpose of root cause analysis, recognize the issues involved in identifying a root cause, and use various tools (e.g., 5 whys, Pareto charts, fault tree analysis, cause and effect diagrams) to resolve chronic problems. (Analyze)

3. *Waste analysis.* Identify and interpret the seven classic wastes (overproduction, inventory, defects, over-processing, waiting, motion, transportation) and resource under-utilization. (Analyze)

VII. Improve (21 Questions)

A. *Design of experiments (DOE)*

1. *Terminology.* Define basic DOE terms, e.g., independent and dependent variables, factors and levels, response, treatment, error, nested. (Understand)

2. *Design principles.* Define and apply DOE principles, e.g., power, sample size, balance, repetition, replication, order, efficiency, randomization, blocking, interaction, confounding, resolution. (Apply)

3. *Planning experiments.* Plan and evaluate DOEs by determining the objective, selecting appropriate factors, responses, and measurement methods, and choosing the appropriate design. (Evaluate)

4. *One-factor experiments.* Design and conduct completely randomized, randomized block, and Latin square designs, and evaluate their results. (Evaluate)

5. *Two-level fractional factorial experiments.* Design, analyze, and interpret these types of experiments, and describe how confounding can affect their use. (Evaluate)

6. *Full factorial experiments.* Design, conduct, and analyze these types of experiments. (Evaluate)

B. *Lean methods*

1. *Waste elimination.* Select and apply tools and techniques for eliminating or preventing waste, e.g., pull systems, kanban, 5S, standard work, poka-yoke. (Analyze)

2. *Cycle-time reduction.* Use various tools and techniques for reducing cycle time, e.g., continuous flow, single-minute exchange of die (SMED), heijunka (production leveling). (Analyze)

3. *Kaizen.* Define and distinguish between kaizen and kaizen blitz and describe when to use each method. (Apply)

4. *Other improvement tools and techniques.* Identify and describe how other process improvement methodologies are used, e.g., theory of constraints (TOC), overall equipment effectiveness (OEE). (Understand)

C. *Implementation.* Develop plans for implementing proposed improvements, including conducting pilot tests or simulations, and evaluate results to select the optimum solution. (Evaluate)

VIII. Control (15 Questions)

A. *Statistical process control (SPC)*

1. *Objectives.* Explain the objectives of SPC, including monitoring and controlling process performance, tracking trends, runs, and reducing variation within a process. (Understand)

2. *Selection of variables.* Identify and select critical process characteristics for control chart monitoring. (Apply)

3. *Rational subgrouping.* Define and apply the principle of rational subgrouping. (Apply)

4. *Control chart selection.* Select and use control charts in various situations: $\bar{X} - R$, $\bar{X} - s$, individual and moving range (ImR), p, np, c, u, short-run SPC, and moving average. (Apply)

5. *Control chart analysis.* Interpret control charts and distinguish between common and special causes using rules for determining statistical control. (Analyze)

B. *Other controls*

1. *Total productive maintenance (TPM).* Define the elements of TPM and describe how it can be used to consistently control the improved process. (Understand)

2. *Visual controls.* Define the elements of visual controls (e.g., pictures of correct procedures, color-coded components, indicator lights), and describe how they can help control the improved process. (Understand)

C. *Maintain controls*

1. *Measurement system reanalysis.* Review and evaluate measurement system capability as process capability improves, and ensure that measurement capability is sufficient for its intended use. (Evaluate)

2. *Control plan.* Develop a control plan to maintain the improved process performance, enable continuous improvement, and transfer responsibility from the project team to the process owner. (Apply)

D. *Sustain improvements*

1. *Lessons learned.* Document the lessons learned from all phases of a project and identify how improvements can be replicated and applied to other processes in the organization. (Apply)

2. *Documentation.* Develop or modify documents including standard operating procedures (SOPs), work instructions, and control plans to ensure that the improvements are sustained over time. (Apply)

3. *Training for process owners and staff.* Develop and implement training plans to ensure consistent execution of revised process methods and standards to maintain process improvements. (Apply)

4. *Ongoing evaluation.* Identify and apply tools (e.g., control charts, control plans) for ongoing evaluation of the improved process, including monitoring leading indicators, lagging indicators, and additional opportunities for improvement. (Apply)

IX. Design for Six Sigma (DFSS) Framework and Methodologies (7 Questions)

A. *Common DFSS methodologies.* Identify and describe DMADV (define, measure, analyze, design, and validate) and DMADOV (define, measure, analyze, design, optimize, and validate). (Understand)

B. *Design for X (DFX).* Describe design constraints, including design for cost, design for manufacturability (producibility), design for test, and design for maintainability. (Understand)

C. *Robust designs*. Describe the elements of robust product design, tolerance design, and statistical tolerancing. (Understand)

LEVELS OF COGNITION—BASED ON *BLOOM'S TAXONOMY—* REVISED (2001)

In addition to *content* specifics, the subtext for each topic in this BoK also indicates the intended *complexity level* of the test questions for that topic. These levels are based on "Levels of Cognition" (from *Bloom's Taxonomy*—Revised, 2001) and are presented below in rank order, from least complex to most complex.

Remember

Recall or recognize terms, definitions, facts, ideas, materials, patterns, sequences, methods, principles, etc.

Understand

Read and understand descriptions, communications, reports, tables, diagrams, directions, regulations, etc.

Apply

Know when and how to use ideas, procedures, methods, formulas, principles, theories, etc.

Analyze

Break down information into its constituent parts and recognize their relationship to one another and how they are organized; identify sublevel factors or salient data from a complex scenario.

Evaluate

Make judgments about the value of proposed ideas, solutions, etc., by comparing the proposal to specific criteria or standards.

Create

Put parts or elements together in such a way as to reveal a pattern or structure not clearly there before; identify which data or information from a complex set is appropriate to examine further or from which supported conclusions can be drawn.

References

Durivage, Mark A. 2014. *Practical Engineering, Process, and Reliability Statistics*. Milwaukee: ASQ Quality Press.

———. 2016. *Practical Design of Experiments (DOE): A Guide for Optimizing Designs and Processes*. Milwaukee: ASQ Quality Press.

———. 2015. *Practical Attribute and Variable Measurement Systems Analysis (MSA): A Guide for Conducting Gage R&R Studies and Test Method Validations*. Milwaukee: ASQ Quality Press.

Graham, Nick, and Stanley E. Portny. 2011. *Project Management for Dummies*. Chichester, West Sussex: John Wiley & Sons.

Kaplan, Robert S., and David Norton. 1992. *The Balanced Scorecard: Measures That Drive Performance*. Harvard Business Review 70, no. 1 (January–February): 71–79. (Reprint #92105.) Available at http://www.hbs.edu/faculty/product/9161.

Williams, Meri. 2008. *Principles of Project Management*. Melbourne: SitePoint.